1

GETTING THE MOST

FROM YOUR DATA

A handbook of practical ideas
on how to analyse qualitative data

Interesting Ways To Teach

In the same series:

Preparing to teach: An introduction to effective teaching in higher education

53 Interesting Things To Do In Your Lectures

53 Interesting Things To Do In Your Seminars And Tutorials

53 Interesting Ways To Assess Your Students

53 Interesting Ways Of Helping Your Students To Study

53 Interesting Communication Exercises For Science Students

53 Interesting Ways To Appraise Your Teaching

53 Interesting Ways To Promote Equal Opportunities In Education

53 Interesting Ways To Teach Mathematics

253 Ideas For Your Teaching

Interesting Ways To Teach: 7 Do-it-yourself Training Exercises

Creating A Teaching Profile

GETTING THE MOST

FROM YOUR DATA

A handbook of practical ideas
on how to analyse qualitative data

Judith Riley

Fellow in Management Education
King's Fund College

Technical and Educational Services Ltd.

First published in 1990 by
Technical and Educational Services Ltd.,
37 Ravenswood Road
Bristol BS6 6BW
UK

ISBN 0 947885 30 7

Printed in Great Britain by Billing & Sons Ltd., Worcester

About Judith Riley

Judith is a Fellow of the King's Fund College which is a charitable organisation providing management development for the National Health Service. She works as a consultant, trainer and researcher with doctors, nurses and managers of various kinds.

Previously she was a senior lecturer at the Open University, in a department that did research on the OU's own educational effectiveness.

This book brings together her interests in adult students, nursing, research methods and helping people to write.

Contents   Page

Is this book for you?

I have written this book for all those who are doing 'soft' research: the kind of research where you collect opinions, observations and wordy statements, rather than numbers. Quantitative numerical data is often called 'hard' data, whereas this book is for people working with 'soft' qualitative data. Qualitative data is often collected by observing people's behaviour, joining in their conversations, or by asking them open-ended questions. The two approaches can, of course, be combined: a qualitative foray in a new area may allow you to develop hypotheses which can then be tested by a quantitative survey.

You may be doing 'soft' research as a student project or as part of your job. Most social science students have to attempt this kind of study and many courses of professional training also insist on such a project. It is also a common approach in research designed to improve public services and in customer relations and marketing in the private sector. So while your study may be assessed by your teachers for an end of term project, it could equally be designed to inform yourself and your working colleagues, rather than any examiners; or, indeed, you may be working for a client. The guidance that I have to offer should be useful, whether you have to prepare a major formal report on your work or are making an informal check which needs no written report at all.

Many of the examples in this book are drawn from the fields of education and health, as that is where I have worked most recently. I first tried qualitative research when I chose to do my doctoral thesis on how academics at the Open University prepared their correspondence texts. I watched them working, drafting alone and discussing courses in team meetings. I interviewed them, asking them to describe what they were doing. I got them to talk into a dictaphone when working at home. Then I had to make sense out of files of notes and boxes full of audio cassettes and write a thesis about my findings.

To give you a contrasting example to that solitary student research, more recently I have been one member of a team of management consultants trying to help members of a health authority to work more effectively. I interviewed each member and wrote notes during each encounter. From these notes I prepared brief biographies for circulation among the members and gave a lecture to the group, giving them feedback about their stated aims, expectations, concerns and strategies.

There are many books on research methodology, both quantitative and qualitative. However, while there is plenty of advice on qualitative research at the level of its philosophy and methodological principles, there is little about the nitty gritty of handling the data. Studies based on interviews and observation are notably thin on descriptions of how the categories and findings were discovered. There is no parallel in qualitative research for the quantitative workers many practical guides to the various statistical procedures involved and how to present numerical results. This book fills that gap for the 'soft' researcher.

This book is about analysing your data: it does not try to help you to work out how to collect it. However, one of the key points about qualitative research is that you cannot neatly separate data collection from its analysis. You do need some sense of the aims of your project before you plunge too deeply into collecting data. Equally, you may need to return to collect more data if your analysis shows a need for it. There are plenty of good textbooks on how to do this. For example, I have found Glaser and Strauss, 1967 and Guba, 1978 very helpful. Glaser and Strauss, though old, is very clear on the ideal principles behind what you are trying to do. The examples in Guba are mostly from studies of school classrooms, but his explanations of data collection techniques apply to other situations too.

I have written this book because I find 'soft' research stressful as well as fascinating. I always enjoy collecting data, but then get depressed at the task of making sense of what I have got. I have gradually discovered many ways of making analysis easier. The textbooks tell you what you **ought** to be doing to analyse your data and, if you are unsure about this, I suggest that you look at Miles and Huberman, 1984. That book recommends a rigorous process of categorising, analysing and auditing. My problem has always been that even when I know what I ought to be doing, I usually cannot do it! Existing textbooks failed to help me with the creative business of finding meaning and generating new ideas, while most of them also ignore the fact that researchers have feelings. I hope that this book will be both practically helpful and supportive.

I have divided the book into six sections. Each of the first five sections corresponds to a different task in analysis.

* **How to organise your data**

* **How to hear what your data has to say** .

* **How to recognise and pattern your own ideas about your data**

* **How to organise evidence for your interpretation**

* **How to present your findings**

The last section is concerned with **selecting techniques**.

To some extent these are in chronological order, starting with organising the raw data and ending with writing a report. However, you will probably find that you behave in a more spiral fashion, revisiting some tasks several times, doubling back to develop an idea in more detail. To help you to dip in I have begun each technique on a new page and given them all the same set of sub-headings.

* **Example.**

* **Why you might want to do it.**

* **How to do it.**

Each of the first five main sections has an introduction, which is probably worth reading before looking at any particular tip. The introductions are organised under the following headings.

* **What are you trying to do?**

* **What is this going to be like?**

* **How can you cope?**

There is a glossary immediately after this preface to help you to check any unfamiliar terms.

This book is not comprehensive. It began as a joint venture with a colleague, Elizabeth Beaty, collecting all the tips that we and our friends had found useful. I am most grateful for her help; without that joint work at the beginning this book would never have happened. We began by asking our immediate colleagues how they had analysed their qualitative data in recent projects. My thanks to them for this information: to Angie Ballard, Beryl Crookes, Diana Laurillard and Fred Lockwood. I am also grateful to the John Davidson, Trevor Habeshaw and Adrian Shaw for their editorial and graphic design support. If you know of any other things that have helped you to enjoy the analysis of qualitative research, I would be very pleased to hear from you too.

References
B. G. Glaser & A. L. Strauss   *The Discovery of Grounded Theory*
Aldine, New York, 1967.

E.G. Guba   *Toward a Methodology of Naturalistic Inquiry in Educational Evaluation*
Univ. of California at Los Angeles Press, 1978.

M. B. Miles & A. M. Huberman   *Qualitative Data Analysis*
Sage, California, 1984.

Glossary

There is no firm agreement among qualitative researchers on terminology. The following explanations do not attempt to be tight definitions, but they should help you to understand how I have used these words in this book.

Audience	The people who want the results of your work: employers, colleagues, examiners or unknown future readers of any report you write.
Brainstorm	A way to generate useable ideas or solutions to problems by encouraging the flow of uncensored suggestions in a relaxed but purposeful atmosphere.
Category	The smallest grouping of data to which you give a name.
Client	A paying or controlling audience.
Code	A referencing system added to a section of data. It usually summarises reference information (see below) but can also indicate the categories to which you have assigned the data.
Data	Raw information in any form, such as observation notes or recorded conversations, before analysis.
Findings	The overall meaning of your work, usually expressed as descriptive and interpretive statements.
Hard data	See *quantitative data.*
Informant	Anyone providing data, including both those who know they are being studied and those you observe without their knowledge.
Interpretation	A personal view of the meaning and significance of data or a situation.
Messages	The few main points in an interpretation.
Negative instances	Bits of data that contradict your interpretation.
Observation	The process of collecting data by looking rather than hearing.
Open-ended questions	Questions which cannot be answered with a simple yes or no but instead provoke a lengthy response in your participants own words.
Participant	An informant who has been told about your study and has agreed to help you.
Pattern	A shape or story that seems to link together several of your interpretive points.

Qualitative data	Data that cannot readily be summarised in the form of numbers. It is often recorded as words, but may include sounds, pictures or other materials. Qualitative studies are usually also open-ended exploratory case studies.
Quantitative data	Data that can be summarised in numbers, often counts of the numbers of informants who make each choice of pre-set answers in a survey. Quantitative studies are usually surveys designed to test hypotheses with a sample of informants.
Reference information	Information about the source of data, such as the name of the informant and the date and place of the record.
Reliability	The extent to which another person who had seen and heard what you did would have recorded the same data.
Repertory Grid	A technique which aims to discover the terms (usually called 'constructs') in which an individual views the social world.
Respondent	A participant who talks or writes to you.
Soft data	See qualitative data.
Supervisor	A teacher who is responsible for helping students to achieve a good standard of work.
Survey	A quantitative research technique, usually asking a series of questions of a group of people. It is often done by post using a questionnaire.
Validity	The extent to which your data record the significant features of the situation that you are studying.

How to organise your data

1   Coding tapes
2   Making transcripts
3   Multiple copies to cut up
4   Punched cards
5   Using a micro-computer
6   Contents lists
7   Linear codes down the margin
8   Coding paragraphs
9   Highlighting text
10   Adding your own comments

How to organise your data

What are you trying to do?

Data is raw information in any form, before it has been analysed. Most of the examples I use in this book refer to data in the form of audio-cassettes and notes. Sometimes these record real events: a cassette running throughout a meeting or my notes of how people behaved while doing a piece of work. Sometimes they record more contrived material such as interviews I've held with my informants. Sometimes they include my own thoughts and feelings while making these observations. You may have other forms of data: lists, tables, diagrams, video cassettes, letters, diaries or official documents.

So that you can analyse the data you have collected, you want it to be accessable and manageable. This means identifying topics within your data; putting it into a form where you can mess about with it without destroying it; organising, lableing or indexing it so that you can find particular sections whenever you need them.

More specifically you need to do six things:
* Turn your data into a form that can be easily studied and copied. For example, making transcripts of audio-cassettes.

* Add reference information to the data. For example, putting a list of who was present on the top of all your notes of meetings.

* Make summaries of the contents of your data.

* Identify and mark potentially interesting sections of data that you may want to return to later.

* Record your initial reactions to the data

* Develop a filing and storage system.

What is this going to be like?

Most qualitative data is interesting and you may find yourself fascinated by your records, reading over your notes and listening to cassettes with great pleasure.

The worst feeling at this stage is of being swamped. Your desk is covered with cassettes and you are not sure that you know which is which. Your bookshelf is groaning with files of notes which you cannot bear to open. You may feel completely overwhelmed and disorganised. You are probably aware of a danger of losing ideas in your sea of data, even of losing some of the data itself.

When you are coding and filing your data you will probably find that you feel bored. You may feel as though you are doing mindless manual labour.

However, you may also feel safe. Later, when you feel a bit better organised, you may find that you feel reluctant to let go and move on to interpretation. You can see gaps in your data or perhaps you feel that there is just nothing very startling in it. Either way, beware. Ask yourself how you can be sure these are genuine problems. Ask yourself if you are worried about your ability to interpret and so may be delaying analysis.

How can you cope?

The essential strategies are to begin early and to do the minimum. Beginning early means that you start organising your data with the very first note or tape. It doesn't seem to matter if your first attempts are not very successful and have to be changed; but it is crucial to put basic reference information on every item and then start sorting the first few items. If you wait till you have a lot of data you will feel swamped when you come to devising the best possible system for filing it.

Doing the minimum is also an important strategy, because you must start sorting the data before you have it all clear in your mind. You can waste days on an elaborate filing system which proves useless later. A rule I found useful was never to do more than about half a day of organising without going on to a deeper level of analysis. I only returned to coding when I was sure that I had an interest in that piece of data. For example, in one study I collected a lot of notes of meetings and tape-recordings, as well as individual interviews. I wasted quite a lot of time organising all this material before I realised that, while the interview data was a rich source and my notes of meetings were useful, the tapes of meetings were poor sources for my study. I needed transcripts of the interviews, with lots of reference information and categorisation of each paragraph. I picked up some additional categories from my notes, and needed reference information for where those occurred.

However, when it came to the tapes of the meetings, I simply stuck a label on each with its date and main topic. Since I didn't need his data at all and left it in that format and uncoded. That said, you may need to return to organising such data at the end of your study.

It could help to have a quick think at this stage about how you are going to present your findings. In particular, if you can get an idea of how you are going to include any data in your presentation, you may see certain kinds of data that are worth marking now.

You may decide later that you need to get another person to code your data independently (Item 37: *Using a second categoriser*). However, that need not affect your determination to do the minimum at this stage in the analysis.

All this assumes that you have got some useful data and want to do some analysis. However, you may feel pretty sure that you asked the wrong questions or your informants have told you nothing interesting. The only solution may be to start again, but do protect your pride by calling your first attempt a pilot! If you are a student, it may be better to put your energy into criticising your existing data. It is worth getting your teacher's advice on this, for examiners can be very impressed by students who can discuss their research methods critically.

Summary

Aims	- Make data easy to study and copy. - Add essential reference information. - Make initial contents summaries. - Identify sections to return to. - Record own reactions to the data. - Develop a filing and storage system.
Feelings	Fascinated by your data. Swamped by so much data. Fear of losing data. Boredom with routine tasks. Safe with routine tasks.
Strategies	Begin early. Do the minimum.
Techniques	Coding tapes. Making transcripts. Multiple copies to cut up. Punched cards. Using a micro-computer. Content lists. Linear codes down the margin. Coding paragraphs. Highlighting text. Adding your own comments.

1   Coding tapes

Example

I am going to interview a speech therapist about her work, planning to record the conversation on a small cassette recorder. I start the cassette at home and say into the microphone,

'This cassette belongs to Judith Riley at the King's Fund College. It is the 13th May, 1988. What follows is an interview with Sheila Smith about her job at the Southview Hospital.'

I also write a small label and stick it on the cassette before the interview. It looks like this:

When I get back after the interview, I add this interview to a list of my accumulating data cassettes: *no.6: S.S. interview, 13/05/88*

Why you might want to do it.

It is surprising how quickly one can forget the details of a recording, particularly if you make several in one day; or if you leave a tape for a while before trying to analyse its contents. You cannot tell what a cassette is about at a glance, as you can with written data (Item 2: *Making transcripts*). While you do not want to spend too much time on 'housekeeping', it is essential to make a note of some minimum information, and in a way that cannot get separated from the cassette.

How to do it.

You need to decide what reference information you need. Commonly you would want:
*   Dates and possibly times for each piece of data.

*   Which informants are speaking.

*   The place of the recording.

You might also want to make a note of the type of data, such as: interview, conversation, diary tape, recording of parts of a meeting, your own thoughts. If you are likely to lose a cassette, you might add information on how to return it to you if found.

The easiest method is to put this information on a small sticky label directly on each cassette that you use. However, there is not much room and you may need to devise some sort of shorthand and keep a key to its meaning on a separate sheet of paper. For example, I used 'S.S.' in the example above to represent my informant's name, Sheila Smith.

It is probably better to STICK THE COMPLETED LABEL ON BEFORE YOU MAKE A RECORDING and then change it if necessary. That way you won't find yourself with a pile of anonymous cassettes to identify later on. It can help to SPEAK THE INFORMATION ONTO THE TAPE AS WELL in case the label falls off. If you prefer, you could run a couple of silent minutes off and then fill these in after the recording has been made, but I have found that I often forget to do this.

Some kind of a master sheet is also useful, where you note the use of each cassette. If you can afford to have a separate cassette for each recording occasion, that makes things simpler. If you put several different items on a single cassette it can be difficult to find any one item later on. Sometimes a recording has several discrete parts, such as different speakers or subjects under discussion. You may want to save time on analysis by making a note of these changes. If you use a play-back machine with a revolution counter you can note the number where each item starts, either on its sticky label, or on your master list. Without this facility, you can note the length of time each item lasts, or mark the plastic cover to show roughly how fat the reel is at the start of a each item.

Another method of doing this is to allocate a <u>number</u> to all new tapes and to try to keep a record of how they are then used. If you set up a sub-sequence for a particular job, you can easily use sticky spots to indicate that 'Tape 3 = Tape 21'.

2   Making transcripts

Example

If you have recorded a series of meetings on video-cassettes, you might want to make a written record from them and then use that transcript later (with shot-listing and/or numerical references from the machines rev counter) as the basis for much of your analysis.

Why you might want to do it.

Most of the techniques to help you analyse your data need to be done on paper copies. This is because you cannot see the whole, or one part and then immediately another part, on a cassette. You cannot cut up a tape and refile it with bits of another tape at all easily. Nor can you add reference information or your own developing thoughts directly onto sections of a cassette.

However, making transcripts is hugely time-consuming and not to be done lightly. You also lose information, such as expressions, positions or tones of voice, however carefully you try to describe them in words or diagrams.

How to do it.

The first decision is how much of the cassette material is to be transcribed. It is possible to do some analysis directly from cassettes, although it is much more difficult. The criteria to consider are as follows.

* What access do you have to replay facilities? You need somewhere quiet, where you can think and where no-one will be disturbed by you replaying a section many times.

* How much of the material on cassette is relevant and central to your study? Can you treat it as illuminative background, in which case you need not make transcripts, or is this your main data which you need to analyse in detail?

When you are transcribing, it is important to WRITE THE ACTUAL WORDS SPOKEN BY YOUR INFORMANTS, however repetitive, slangy or ungrammatical. Speech is different from written language and your data may well be queried, and your readers will be much less intrigued, if your informants seem to speak like BBC announcers. You need to note basic reference information as you go along and to add any background noises and note movements or facial expressions if you can see or remember these. So you might need a convention, such as curly brackets for example, to add notes such as: {smiling} or {getting up}.

Leave wide margins around the text in case you want to add reference information or other comments. You will probably find that you begin real analysis while you are transcribing. In listening to cassettes you begin to think about what you are hearing and to have ideas about it. These may be no more than questions or comments: 'Surely she can't have meant that?' or 'That's odd, that contradicts what he said before'. These are worth adding to the transcript as you go along as described in Item 10: *Adding your own comments*.

3   Multiple copies to cut up

Example

I had a series of tape-recorded conversations with about 10 academics about how they went about writing. I made transcripts of each conversation and added reference information to every page. Then I made a photo-copy of each page and filed the original copies away. I cut up the copy by the topics we had been talking about, such as: starting writing, writer's block, redrafting. I labelled an old A4 envelope for each of these topics and piled the little slips of paper into these, in no particular order. When I came to analyse this data later I dealt with one envelope at a time, taking out all its slips and sorting them to see what points my informants had made about 'writer's block' etc.

Later in the analysis I made a second set of copies. I cut up my second set in a different way, because I was now looking for other kinds of ideas, ideas about the factors that seemed to be motivating my authors.

Why you might do this.

The big problem with this approach is that you lose the context for each remark or observation that you isolate with your scissors. It helps if you have a good memory so that you can remember contexts. Photo-copying is expensive and if your data is on cassettes it has to be transcribed onto paper.

The aim of the cutting up is to let you resort the data into a different order; to let you put together all the points made about a topic. Then you can look at them together, without being distracted by all the intervening data in the original material.

How to do it.

The most crucial point is DO NOT CUT UP YOUR ONLY COPY.

The second important point is DO NOT CUT UP ANYTHING TILL YOU HAVE PUT REFERENCE INFORMATION ON IT. Item 7: *Linear codes down the margin* suggests a way of adding reference information that is not lost by cutting up. You might also add the page and paragraph numbers on the back of each slip, or code down the edge of the pages so that however you cut you can get back to the original to locate an extract.

It is quicker to make several copies at once, but expensive, so you may prefer just to make a single copy as you need it. You will need to check that your photo-copier has included any marginal codes and notes and that any use of colour is still clear or repeated on the photocopy.

When you begin to accumulate a pile of items on one topic, you can often see that there are really two or three rather different topics being included; you may be able to use those subdivisions from then on. It is common to have between six and thirty separate piles.

You need to decide too whether you are just snipping out apparently important sections, such as telling remarks, or whether you are going to put every line of data into a category. Much depends on whether you feel your informant had a lot to say or kept to the point. If you are sure that much of it is irrelevant, there is little point in struggling to categorise it all and then letting it clutter up your new filing system. For example, while ostensibly telling me about their views on the acute hospital, some health authority members would digress onto whether we should have a cup of coffee and where had I parked my car! I did do a mental check on whether refreshments and car parking were important topics for my study before deciding not to analyse those sections of the data. Equally, you can cut down the work by selecting only certain informants or certain occasions for cutting up. In a big project, where I had transcripts of about 30 hour-long interviews, I chose to copy and cut up only about one quarter of my data. There was probably good material in the other interviews, but I had neither the time nor patience to do any more.

You will also need to decide how big your cut-up slips should be. As a rough guide, less than a couple of lines is rarely sufficient, and more than half a page is likely to be too long. Very small sections are hard to understand later when you come to reread them out of context, and very long sections are usually too diverse to be easily comprehensible.

As you collect little piles of slips of paper for each topic, you need to find them a filing system, such as my old envelopes in the example above.

4   Punched cards

Example.

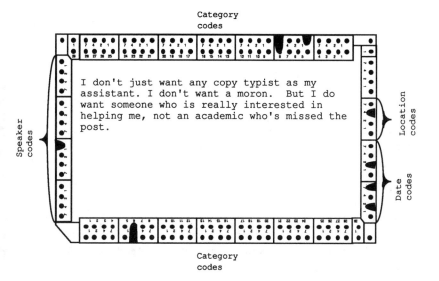

The card illustrated here shows a paragraph cut from a photocopied section of data, from a study of the employment of variously qualified research assistants. The paragraph has been stuck onto a punched card. The data has been coded in various ways which are expressed as slots round the edges.

I don't want just any copy typist as my assistant. I don't want a moron. But I do want someone who is really interested in helping me, not an academic who's missed the post.

Why you might want to do it.

Punched cards offered an advance on ordinary little filing cards when they were first used in the 1940's. They are useful where the researcher needs to count the instances of particular combinations of codes. Having counts of categories can be very useful if you need to satisfy an audience who are used to quantitative data. Item 38: *Counting instances* will help you to get started with this. The great advantage punched cards offer over using a word processor is that, as you can stick sections of data onto each card, you do not have to retype it.

Punched cards were being recommended by some of the experts in qualitative methodology as late as 1980, so I have included this technique here. However, punched cards are not easy to find these days and are expensive to buy. UNLESS YOU ARE FASCINATED BY THIS OLD RESEARCH TECHNIQUE I WOULD NOT USE IT. I find it hard to imagine a set of data that could not be sorted and counted quicker by other methods.

How to do it.

First you have to buy a supply of edge punched cards, such as Cope Chat cards. Try a big stationers. You will also need a few narrow knitting needles, special punched card needles, or thick lengths of wire. You can make the edge nicks with scissors, but it is easier to use a special punch. Computer sorted cards, which look a bit different, were once usable, but the equipment to read them is not now readily available.

Make a photocopy of all the data that you want to put on the cards. If you knew that you were going to use punched cards, you would have made your line lengths short enough to make it possible to cut the material up into sections that are small enough to go onto the centre of a card, without overlapping any of the holes. Usually it helps to split different speakers' statements between separate cards, even if they are very short. If one speaker changes topic, it is probably best to divide his or her words between separate cards.

Each hole on the card can be used for a different item of information. You might use some of the holes to represent your informants, some for the date and place of the encounter and some for the topics that seemed to be being raised. As it is difficult to mend the slots once you have cut them, you should only use topics that you feel fairly sure will not need amending.

When you have a big stack of these sections of data coded in this way, you use the needles to pick out particular selections of cards. For example, suppose you want to know what a particular speaker said about differently qualified research assistants. You put one needle through the holes in the stack which relate to that speaker and another needle through the hole relating to 'research assistants'. When you lift the stack up by the needles and shake it the cards you want, since they have been clipped, will drop out. You can use one needle to free off all the speaker's cards, then use it again to release those on which he or she refers to research assistants. Notice that the cards in the stack can be in any order.

You can copy some of the advantages of the punched card system my marking points along the edges of file cards with colour markers. This enables you to go straight to the cards you want in much the same way.

5   Using a micro-computer

Example.

In a study of managers' difficulties in dealing with all the papers that they have to read, I might have audio-cassettes recording a series of group discussions of the problems. My secretary types these and mails the file to my word processor. I use the search facility to find and print out all the examples of the use of the following words or phrases, which suggest problems with the speed of reading:

slow
fast
speed
speed-read
speed-reading
too much
so much

I might have got three pages of paragraphs which included my chosen words about problems with the speed of reading. I could then go on to look for a further set of examples where the problem was perceived differently, perhaps as indecisiveness over whether to read or ignore a paper.

Why you might want to do it.

If your data has to be typed and you have access to a micro-computer, you can locate particular words or phrases very readily. This can be particularly quick if you can identify categories by words that your informants actually use. If you need to identify and label your own categories, these can be added to the screen quite rapidly. You can use the search and find facility both to identify and count all the instances of particular categories and to find good examples to quote. The instances found are identified with their location in your data files. Sometimes such a search brings up examples that you might not have spotted yourself, because the key words are used in an unusual context.

There is also the great advantage of being able to print out sections of your data, in any order that you choose. Printing out copies can be cheaper than photo-copying. This is particularly useful if you need to make several versions of your findings for different audiences. Make a paper copy of all the data as well, as it is easier to scan as a whole than the large print on the screen.

Obviously, you cannot use a micro if you do not have good access to a machine and a suitable programme. If you have not used a word processor before, you really need someone to help you to deal with the teething problems until you become familiar with this new technique.

Using a micro-computer is not advisable if you can work directly from your hand-written notes; typing in the data is probably unnecessarily time-consuming. Nor would it be sensible if you have less than about thirty pages of data, for that would be quick to scan and there would be few instances of each category. Similarly, if you do not want to count instances, or do not need to produce a typed report incorporating examples of your data, then working directly from paper data may be quicker.

How to do it

You need to check that you have access to the machine and its printer whenever it suits you and that it has a suitable programme. At the time of writing I know of four useful programmes:

* Memory Mate

* Lotus Agenda

* Grandview

* Filemaker II

By the time you read this, there will probably be many more. YOU NEED TO GET ADVICE ON THE MOST SUITABLE.

You have to start by getting your data typed into the machine's files. If you do not have a secretary, I have found that it is quite easy to learn to use a word processor, even though I am a two-finger typist. You need a sympathetic teacher, who will show you the basics and then leave you alone to play with a piece of text in private.

Split up the data into separate files, so that none is longer than about 20 pages of A4 text. Longer files are relatively unmanageable, although this may not be true soon with better machines and programmes. USE THE SAVE FACILITY OFTEN, MAKE WORD PROCESSOR COPIES OF ALL FILES AND KEEP BACK-UP DISKS AND PAPER COPIES TOO! It is very easy to lose a file inside the machine.

You can then use a word search programme to ask the machine to hunt for all mentions of a particular word or phrase in your data. Most search programmes need you to specify plurals and uses of capitals: so 'patient, patients, Patient, Patients, PATIENT, PATIENTS' may all be required. It may help to use a thesaurus to get more ideas for synonyms to include in the search. If you categorise the data yourself, type marginal topic codes into the files, so that you can search for these topics too.

You may need some help with this if you are a beginner. Margins are sometimes hard to get at on a word-processor since they get mixed up with tab points, indents etc. One way round this in the case of the example above is to type **(PATIENT)** at any point you like in the text. You can delete it just before printing if you want a clean copy: it stands out well in the text; it enables you to call up <u>only</u> those examples you have coded, which could be useful with a word like 'patient'!

6   Contents lists

Example.

I have some data about a management course for doctors in the form of a 43 page report from one of the participants. This document has no sections or subheadings at all. I added a contents list on a separate sheet on top:

```
Pages  0 - 7:   Initial feelings

Pages  8 - 29:  Session by session comments

Pages 30 - 41: Discussion of messages

Pages 42 - 43: Practicalities
```

Why you might want to do it.

The idea of contents lists is to give your memory a jog when you return to analysing the data. You may need a brief reminder of each piece of data, without having to listen or read right through it. The more data that you have and the longer the time between collecting it and analysing it, the more useful contents lists become.

How to do it.

There are two useful questions to ask yourself about this:

* What are the main things covered in this data?

* How will I remember this later on?

The important point to remember is that the contents list is very quick to do, just a superficial labelling. It is not a deep interpretation of the meaning of the data. In the example above, the actual value of the data was extracted later in terms of the characteristics of doctors as learners. When I wrote that contents list, I had no idea of what I would find when I thought about the data later on. All I wanted at the categorising stage was to record the most obvious contents of the data, in the order in which they came in the original document.

As a rough guide you might look for something like three or four things to list for each piece of data.

If there is room, you could add this brief list to a label on a cassette, or write it on the top of a section of written data. Another way is to put it on a 3" by 4" index card and clip it to the data. You might like to keep all your contents lists on a separate sheet, along with the basic reference information for each piece of data.

Alternatively, you might like to add such information to the top of each page of data. Just use the top or bottom of your pages to record whatever information you want. As this has to refer to the whole page, it cannot be very detailed. If you write it in the top or bottom right hand corner, you can read it quickly by leafing through the pages.

You can be a bit more sophisticated by using the top of the page for one sort of information, such as who is speaking on this page, and the bottom lines to record something else, such as the main topics.

7 Linear codes down the margin

Example.

The following data is from my study of an Open University team preparing a new multi-media distance education course. The left hand margin has been coded to record who is speaking.

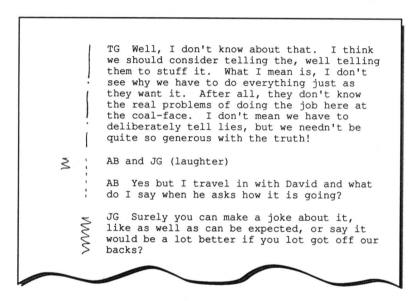

```
TG  Well, I don't know about that.  I think
    we should consider telling the, well telling
    them to stuff it.  What I mean is, I don't
    see why we have to do everything just as
    they want it.  After all, they don't know
    the real problems of doing the job here at
    the coal-face.  I don't mean we have to
    deliberately tell lies, but we needn't be
    quite so generous with the truth!

AB and JG (laughter)

AB  Yes but I travel in with David and what
    do I say when he asks how it is going?

JG  Surely you can make a joke about it,
    like as well as can be expected, or say it
    would be a lot better if you lot got off our
    backs?
```

The list below records some of the line codes used for different speakers in this project.

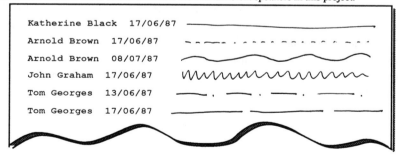

```
Katherine Black  17/06/87
Arnold Brown  17/06/87
Arnold Brown  08/07/87
John Graham  17/06/87
Tom Georges  13/06/87
Tom Georges  17/06/87
```

Why you might want to do this.

One of the easiest ways of beginning to analyse written data is to cut it up according to which topic is mentioned. Then you can look at all the references to any one topic together. You will almost certainly then want to remember who said what, when, in order to assess each point made. Linear codes down the margin prevent you from losing this information from even the smallest section of data. The technique is quick and costs nothing.

However, it does depend on being able to find your key to the various codes!

How to do it.

Start by deciding what you want to code: what information you will need from any piece of data if it gets separated from its source and context later on. In the example above I had put speaker's initials at the start of each speech, but I thought that I might want to divide up some of the longer speeches later, so I wanted the speaker identified throughout his speech. I decided that it might also be useful to attach the date to any fragment too.

I made a list with a different line code for each speaker on each occasion for which I had data. As I had over thirty speaker/occasion combinations, I had to use several different coloured pencils to get enough code lines. You want to choose codes that are quick to draw down the side of a page: straight or wiggly lines are faster than dashed or dotted lines. You need not invent all your line codes at once, you can always add more codes later if you collect more data.

Remember to make yourself a key to the various codes that you choose. If you think that you might lose your key to the codes, MAKE A SPARE LIST and pin it up or file it away.

Alternatively, you could use a different colour of paper on each occasion and keep the different line codes just for identifying the speakers. If you have to use coloured pencils or markers, remember that they may not be distinguishable on a black and white photo-copy. You may then have to re-colour each photocopy. You won't have to imitate the wiggles, dots or dashes. They are on the copy, so merely a coloured line is required. It is good sense always to have an uncut copy before you start snipping! Go through each page of data, adding the appropriate codes down the margin. Turn the pages sideways, if you find that is easier. When you come to cut up the pages, each little slip of paper will carry its own code.

8   Coding paragraphs

Example.

Here is a piece of data from a meeting where several members of a health authority were discussing their working practices. The data has been transcribed from a cassette recording. A quick note of the topics they were discussing has been added in the left hand margin and each speaker has been identified by their initials. I noted the time at one point.

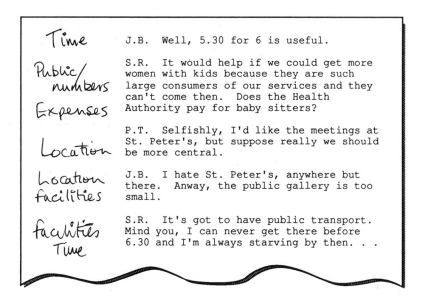

Time	J.B. Well, 5.30 for 6 is useful.
Public/ numbers	S.R. It would help if we could get more women with kids because they are such large consumers of our services and they can't come then. Does the Health
Expenses	Authority pay for baby sitters?
Location	P.T. Selfishly, I'd like the meetings at St. Peter's, but suppose really we should be more central.
Location facilities	J.B. I hate St. Peter's, anywhere but there. Anway, the public gallery is too small.
facilities Time	S.R. It's got to have public transport. Mind you, I can never get there before 6.30 and I'm always starving by then. . .

Why you might want to do it.

As shown in the example above, it is probably best to add the minimum of essential information as soon as possible. However, you should avoid spending hours puzzling to find an appropriate label for every tiny paragraph. As usual, there has to be a warning about spending too long on 'housekeeping'.

When you analyse the data, you may need to know who said what. You will probably need this information if you intend to quote chunks of data in a report on your findings. Additional reference information can help the process of analysis, by letting you trace topics quickly in a mass of data.

How to do it.

Coding in this way assumes that you have broken up your data into a set of paragraphs. It may be worth giving that process a moment's thought first. One easy way is to start a new paragraph each time a different person speaks. In a long speech, you may divide it up into more paragraphs each time they change topic.

You will probably want to identify each speaker by their initials, keeping a list of these separately.

Always leave a good margin so that you can add other information later, if required. For example, in the case above, I recorded the topics under discussion in the left hand margin. I might have added other information, such as the time. If your text is a transcript from a cassette recording, you may want to add notes about background noises or tones of voice. When you start thinking about what your data means, perhaps using some of the tips in the next section of this book, you may well find that you want to add other topic categories in the margin.

9   Highlighting text

Example.

I had a transcript of an interview with an Open University author, on which I highlighted the italicised text.

```
JR  Tell me about the meeting when they discuss
your draft.

AB  Well, you've been there, what did you think?

JR  I wondered what you wanted. . .

AB  Well, you can't just go in and say I want
you to comment on this but nicely, It's my baby
and you can't hit my baby. But that's what you
want really, only to hear the nice things.  In
fact I think that I talk a lot at those meetings
when it's my unit on the block, just kind of,
um. . .  defend it, or defuse kind of. . .

When I took that last unit in, that was so late,
I just started straight in with the Thomas
stuff, there's so much that only I know about
that lot, for example, he found things were a
```

Why you might want to do it.

It is easy to find the highlighted sections again later. Without this kind of help, you can spend hours searching for a point that you remember seemed interesting, or a quotation that you need when you come to write your final report. The pen is cheap, the technique is very quick and highlighter pens usually allow photocopying of the text through the colour. After the first few pages, you can read for other purposes at the same time as watching out for quotable bits.

However, this system does not index the material in any way. It is useful at an early stage in the analysis, when you are looking for ideas. Once you have a complete list of all the concepts that will need illustration, you will probably be better served by a more complex system of coding, such as Item 7: *Linear codes down the margin* or Item 8: *Coding paragraphs.*

How to do it.

Keep to hand a coloured pen, or better still a highlighter pen whenever you are reading through any of your written data. Use the pen to mark the text whenever you feel that you have found something to which you may need to return. N.B. DO NOT MARK YOUR ONLY COPY OF THE DATA. If it is a short phrase, just underline or wash over the significant words. If it is longer, it will be quicker to mark down the side of the text. I have used both conventions above, underlining or washing over the phrase that first caught my eye and later adding a line down the side of a short section that seemed important.

When you begin to use this technique, you will probably need to have a list of criteria for what might be quotable. At first I found that I needed consciously to ask myself about quotability at the end of each page. After a few pages, the whole thing becomes more automatic. Your criteria for quotability might include the following.

* A telling or memorable phrase, that catches the imagination, like 'my baby' in the example above. It might become the name for one of your categories of analysis.

* Something that sums up a section of data or characterises a speaker. Someone might refer to himself or herself as 'a bit of a worrier', for example.

* A particularly clear illustrative example of one of your emerging categories. In the example I had a vague idea of 'defensiveness', which was nicely illustrated by AB likening his draft text to his baby.

* A negative instance, an example that contradicts your ideas. For example, AB might have gone on to say that he liked **certain** kinds of criticism.

* An interesting variant on one of your categories. AB used the word 'defuse' in my example, which could be seen as a variant on my idea of 'defensiveness'.

10   Adding your own comments

Example.

The following section records some data from a conversation with two Health Service managers about their difficulties in coping with the large amounts of reading that they had to do. I took rough notes of the points they made and kept a running commentary of my own thoughts as the conversation developed. I put my thoughts into square brackets and on the right hand side of the page.

```
        Me:   What problems?

        Ray:  Hates it
              Carries it home and back
                             [ Reluctant      ]

        Tom:  So slow
                        [ Beligerent. Shouldn't
                          have to do it.  ]

        Me:   What role reading in jobs?

        Tom:  Used to be none, now loads of bumf
                             [ It's unnecessary? But
                               management different ]
```

Why you might want to do this.

You need a way of capturing your own thoughts near to the data that prompted them. In the example above, I inserted my own reactions at the same time as I made my initial record of the interview. You might also wish to add comments immediately on return to your base. At later stages in the analysis, you will want to read the two together. You must make it clear which are your thoughts and be sure to AVOID CONFUSING THEM WITH YOUR INFORMANTS' IDEAS.

How to do it.

You need ways of adding comments at three different times:

* During data collection.
* When transcribing a cassette onto paper.
* When reading through later.

If you collect data onto cassettes, you will probably need to keep a written note of points that you want to add. If your data is written, then you need a convention to distinguish your additions. You can put your notes in a different standard location: such as always in the right hand margin, or on the back of the previous sheet, or insert separate sheets of paper for them. Or you can use a symbol, such as my square brackets in the example above. It is a bit fiddly to use a different pen.

All this points yet again to the desirability of leaving wide margins. If you have time, draw lines down the page, using a strip of about half a page width in the centre for the record and the remaining margins for different types of comment or annotation.

If you make transcripts of cassette data, you can add your comments from your separate notes at that stage, using placing or symbols to distinguish your own thoughts from your informants' speech.

Personally , I now automatically use the convention of square brackets shown in the example, but I often run out of space for subsequent notes. One solution to this has been the use of the back of each sheet for later additions. Whatever strategy you adopt, DO NOT LET YOUR COMMENTS DEFACE THE ORIGINAL RECORD.

How to hear what your data has to say

How to hear what your data has to say

What are you trying to do?

The aim is to be able to describe your data, to summarise it, to pull out the main points and to begin to develop categories.

For some studies this may even be the final stage of the work, although most of you will probably want to go on to some kind of interpretation of your description. You want to become so familiar with your data that you can find your way around it easily and answer any questions about it without hesitation.

This is also the stage at which you need to begin to think about evidence: how are you going to support your descriptive summary? This is not so much a matter of proving anything, as of bringing a flavour of audit into your approach. Section 4 makes specific suggestions about how to do this.

At this stage, you need to try to put aside your existing knowledge of the topic you are studying, what you have learned about other researchers' ideas. You will need these hypotheses later on, but for the best description you need to focus on your data alone. The idea is to try really to hear what your own data have to say. It may be subtly different from others' findings.

What is this going to be like?

This can be a very good stage in the work: you may almost fall in love with your data. You may well find that you thoroughly enjoy reading or listening to it; that you feel enthusiastic. Indeed one of the problems is that you may enjoy this phase so much that you cannot make yourself move on to complete the work.

However, even if you enjoy exploring your data, you may find this stage quite stressful, because there is too much of it. You may feel lost in the trees and unable to describe the wood. You may be overwhelmed by your own thoughts about the data, fleeting ideas that may tumble out so fast that you cannot catch them. You may find it terribly hard to put existing theories aside and concentrate on your own data. You may feel overwhelmed by the 'if only' syndrome: if only I had asked that extra question or talked to a few more informants.

So, how can you cope?

The essential strategy is to **immerse yourself in your data**. This takes time, but it need not be big blocks of time. Take sections of data with you wherever you go, play interview cassettes in the car, read bits of transcripts while waiting for buses, mull over your notes of characters when you have to sit through boring meetings. You might aim to look at all your data at least twice and some interesting sections many more times.

You don't just have to read or listen to your data and then put it down and write a description. That would be very hard. Experienced researchers use a strategy of **repetition** to help them to study their own data. You can read or listen, take a long section all at one go or just a few sentences at a time, read silently or aloud. You can also try different focuses in each repetition: looking for transcript errors and possible additions, thinking about your own reactions at the time of data collection. You might listen to an audio cassette which recorded a meeting and then transcribe parts of it, which involves listening to it again. You might read the transcript through once quickly and then again more slowly, checking it against the cassette recording and adding your own thoughts from the notes that you made at the time of the recording. You might read that aloud slowly, thinking about what the transcript tells you about your area of interest. Later, after some other work has given you a fresh outlook, you might return and listen to the cassette again to see how it strikes you now.

This strategy of **distancing** can be very helpful. If you just sit down and run through the same piece of data again and again, you will soon get bored and become unable really to listen to it. Break up the repetitions with doing other things, let some time pass and come back to the data another day. You want to be completely familiar with your data so that you are able to describe it and go on to think about it.

The final strategy is to **select techniques** that suit you and your study. It is most unlikely that you will need to try all my suggestions.

Summary

Aims	- Make summary decription. - Become familiar with your data. - Identify categories of points. - Enable an appropriate sense of audit.
Feelings	Enthusiastic emjoyment. Lost in the quantity of data. Overwhelmed by ideas. Regrets over your data's imperfections.
Strategies	Immerse yourself in your data. Repetition. Distancing. Select techniques.
Techniques	Go back and get more data. Writing summaries. Looking for common points. Reading aloud. Looking for surprises. Concentrating on a single instance. Listening in roles. Annotating the record.

11 Returning for more data

Example.

When listening to a taped record of a conversation with one of your informants, you realise that you cannot hear some of her answers. Maybe you interrupted her, or there was background noise, or you have a faulty cassette. In addition, you cannot understand quite what she meant by one remark. This often happens if you were concentrating on guiding the conversation rather than listening to your informant. If these gaps seem important, then it makes sense to go back for another try.

Why you might want to do it.

Textbooks give firm advice that qualitative research should be reiterative and that data collection and analysis should go hand in hand as parallel tasks. This means that you should not wait until you have completed the fieldwork before starting to think about what you have got. It is only as you begin to grasp the shape of your data that you can see clearly what informants and situations you need to study. They call it 'progressive focussing'. If you do too much data collection before analysing it you will certainly find that you have wasted a lot of effort, for much of it will be repetitive. The solution usually lies in 'having to stop somewhere' and in balancing time and effort against the established priorities of the project - two decisions which are not always easy to arrive at.

Returning to data collection should therefore be a carefully planned business. In practice I find that I always collect too much data: every study ends with an embarrassing pile of notes or cassettes that I file and then never look at again. However, I did at least think about <u>all</u> of it at the time of collection. Hence, even if I did not analyse it all fully, iI was able to use it to guide my general thoughts on the subject in hand.

How to do it.

It usually makes sense to wait until you have had a look at quite a lot of your data before rushing off for more. Otherwise you may find that you need to make more than one return trip. Most informants are happy to be visited again, if you can find a time and place that suits them. Another reason for waiting a while before going back for more is that you may think of new topics that you did not cover in the original interview. On a return visit, you may be able to ask more pointed questions. Or you can ask whether your informant has had any more thoughts since you last met.

There is no right time to stop collecting data, no way of knowing whether you have enough, no statistical test of the adequacy of your sample size. My advice is to REMEMBER THAT YOU ARE MAKING A CASE STUDY AND BE WARY ABOUT RETURNING. It is easy to spend too much time collecting data, leaving insufficient time for analysis. You may end up overloaded with data. Ask yourself questions such as the following.

* Can I expect to learn anything new from returning?

* Do I need to elaborate any of these initial notes?

* Do I want to return just to be tidy?

* Am I returning to please my informants?

* Am I avoiding moving on to analysis?

12   Writing summaries

Example.

You have twelve transcripts of interviews with midwives about their work. You write a two side summary of each, including any quotations from the data that seem particularly striking. You read each of the summaries several times and then make a further precis of those twelve double pages. This final precis might be only three pages long. You then do all your initial analysis of your data by working with those twelve summaries and the precis, not returning to your original transcripts at all.

Why you might want to do it.

This is a powerful tool for making your data more manageable. You can save an enormous amount of time by working with condensed versions of your data. Summaries make it much easier to get an overview and to think about your data as a whole, provided that they are not too extensive. I find that I always use this technique even if my original data is only a few tens of pages of notes. In making the summaries I seem to move forward a stage in the process of becoming familiar with my data: it forces me to get to grips with the main points.

However, summarising has its disadvantages. You are bound to lose some potential ideas if you abandon the fullness of the original data. You may be tempted to rely on your summaries for too long and never check your emerging analysis with reality, or even your first-hand notes of reality. You may get bored if you do most of the thinking around your own words, at two removes from your field situations and your informants' own turns of phrase.

It can be quite time-consuming to make summaries of a lot of data unless you are particularly skilled at writing them quickly. If you have more than about 100 pages of data you probably need to use the technique selectively.

How to do it.

Everyone has their own way of preparing summaries. One way that works for me is to start by reading the data several times. Then I start to read it again but this time I jot down each point as I come to it, in just two or three words. My final step is to work from those brief phrases alone. You might find it helpful, in seeing the wood for the trees, to use Item 24: *Letters to friends* or Item 25: *Conversations.*

13   Looking for common points

Example.

You might have observations of annual appraisal interviews. When you study your notes, one of the questions you ask yourself is 'How did the employees react?' You can find four different reactions in the first few interviews:

become angry
become defensive
avoid
ignore

Looking at what these had in common, you might call them all 'negative reactions to criticism'. This helps you to look for some positive reactions as well and you find these in your data from some later interviews. Later in the analysis you group both positive and negative reactions along with other categories in a major section of your report called 'forming standards'.

Why you might want to do it.

Forming lists of possible categories of points lies at the heart of describing your data. They will form the building blocks for your description. In thinking about names for categories, I have often found I begin to see themes that stay throughout the analysis.

How to do it .

In the end a report is often going to draw general conclusions from specific data. This may well involve turning incidents into generalisations and grouping ideas to form concepts.

These differences which you to see the data with fresh eyes. So, in the example above, you would not choose as headings the items from the agendas of the meetings, because that would produce straight summaries of your minutes. It may help to identify good headings if you ask yourself some of the following questions.

*   What different kinds of activities were going on? Think of what people were trying to achieve and the real effects of what people said, as well as what they did.

*   What different kinds of topics came up repeatedly?

* What different kinds of people were present? Think about their actual functions or roles, rather than their official titles.

* What kinds of factors seemed to be influencing behaviours? Think about what might be motivating your informants.

* What kinds of explanations are they offering? For example, do they appeal to tradition and precedent, or to some idea about what they ought to be doing, or to what is convenient?

* What are they assuming?

Do not worry over the choice of a name for a category at this stage, anything that you understand will do for now; you can change the 'working name' later. Eventually you will try to achieve names which meet the following criteria.

* Single words or short phrases
* Preferably using your informants' own words
* Memorable, catchy
* Covers all the examples you have in mind
* Has appropriate associations, especially not derogatory!
* Fits with your other categories' names to form a coherent set

It is hard to say how many categories you should find. Less than six categories in all seems a bit thin for any study, more than thirty might well be excessive.

After your initial categories are beginning to become clear, see if you can group them in any way. It may help to think of having two or three levels of categories. In my example above I would call 'anger' a first level of category, 'negative reactions to criticisms' the next level up, and 'forming standards' a third level.

14   Reading aloud

Example.

On going out for a walk you take with you your notes from observing six occupational therapists at work. When you have found somewhere suitably secluded, you read them aloud. Then it occurs to you that all of your participants smiled at their patients and asked them about something personal in a caring attentive way. You realise that it could be worth considering whether occupational therapists have a series of stages that they go through with each patient, and that the first stage might be something like 'Making friends' or 'Allaying fears'.

Why you might want to do it.

Reading aloud seems to help concentration, so that you do not get to the bottom of the page with no memory of what you have just read. It slows you down and helps the data to seem less familiar.

On the other hand, you may find that you feel embarrassed, declaiming to the air, and so your concentration is destroyed. Try it if you find it hard to concentrate when reading silently, or as a way of varying this stage of the analysis.

How to do it.

Find a place where you can be sure that no-one will overhear you. Read aloud slowly and clearly, as though you had an audience. If you can remember the intonations or pauses used by your informants, try to reproduce them. If it is your notes that you are reading, try to read them with some expression, with pauses and emphases and different tones of voice. Listen to yourself. PAUSE EVERY PAGE OR SO TO THINK ABOUT WHAT YOU HAVE HEARD, not just what words you have read out, but what they now seem to signify.

WRITE DOWN WHAT HAS COME TO MIND, on the margin or on a separate note that you can clip to the relevant pages of data.

15   Looking for surprises

Example.

You have decided that your informants have three attitudes to working overtime:

> *a necessary part of this job*
> *of all jobs*
> *devised by the bosses to annoy them.*

Then you realise that one person is implying a fourth attitude which is much more positive: they seem to see overtime as an indication of how much their work is needed. This view is not just a fourth category of attitude to overtime: in being positive rather than negative it opens up a whole new way of looking at job satisfaction and how attitudes to work are formed.

Why you might want to do it.

Surprises should help you to elaborate and define the main points in your data, to detail the descriptive categories that you are finding. Looking for surprises can be a useful gauge of your familiarity with your data; it can indicate when you are ready to move on from descriptive analysis. Many of the surprising phrases may be useful later when you have to make a final report on your findings, as decribed in Item 41: *Using quotations.*

You may also need a count of instances, as in Item 38, which contradict your interpretation when you come to organise the evidence for your findings.

If you try this technique too early, before you have much idea of what is in your data, too much will surprise you. You need to have a reasonably clear idea of what to expect first, otherwise you may want to note every sentence as remarkable!

How to do it.

I have found it easiest to have a special way of marking surprises, so that I can distinguish them from other annotations on a piece of data. You can use a particular colour of highlighter pen, or a coloured crayon to underline the point, or something like a big star in the margin. One of my colleagues used to copy out surprising phrases onto separate cards, as she found that she often used them as quotations in her final report.

Look for the following.

* Negative instances that contradict an idea that you feel is generally true of your data.

* Boundary instances that show the limits of one of your ideas.

* Ideal instances that sum up an idea remarkably neatly.

* Oddities unexpected remarks or behaviours that you cannot quite understand.

* Phrases that alter your perception of your data, that tell you something about your own assumptions about your data.

It can help to ask yourself questions such as:

* What did he do that I did not expect?

* What did she omit to say that I would have expected her to say?

* Does this behaviour fit my ideas exactly?

* What is there to think about in this data?

Do not expect to find surprises in every section of your data. The more that you are immersed in it and able to describe it, the fewer things will surprise you.

16   Concentrating on a single instance

Example.

You have been studying personnel managers' attitudes to training. You have interviewed sixteen people and have several pages of notes from each interview. You take just one of these sets of notes and begin by using Item 14: *Reading aloud* to get familiar with this material. Then you try Item 13: *Looking for common points* and finally Item 15: *Looking for surprises*. You only move on to reading your other sets of notes when you have extracted as much as possible from exploring the single interview.

Why you might want to do it.

In most analyses of data, researchers are looking for patterns across instances. However, it can be difficult to see common points in a large amount of data and you get bored by the magnitude of the task. Taking a single instance and studying it in depth can be very interesting, as well as giving you ideas for your wider analysis. It is a useful thing to try if you are getting bored with your analysis.

Alternating between concentrating on a single instance and looking more widely at your data can be very helpful. Looking at a small section of data can result in lists of points which need to be checked for incidence across all your data. You could say that looking vertically demands horizontal checking. When you have that horizontal view, it can help to return to looking vertically at a single instance to see how it illustrates points in more detail.

However, there are obvious disadvantages in *starting* with one instance. You may choose an atypical piece of data, in which case your analysis of it will confuse your subsequent work on the rest of the material. In depth analysis can be too absorbing, so that you keep repeating vertical looks at single instances and neglect to look at the full spread of your material.

How to do it.

Choose a piece of data that is expressed in just a few pages of notes or transcript. Choose something that seems interesting, because you are going to spend quite a bit of time on it and you want your efforts to be rewarded with lots of ideas.

Use a selection of the techniques described in this section to explore your chosen piece of data. Write up what you can see in this one piece of data. This will give you some practice in writing descriptions and may provide you with a detailed case study for your final report.

17   Listening in roles

Example.

I had some data on teamwork among academics. I tried looking at my data from the point of view of Eric, my supervisor; Anne, a friend in another faculty who was interested in a related topic; and Ben, an acquaintance from another college who was an expert in applying qualitative methods in educational research.

When I thought about their views I predicted that Eric would be interested in the content of the team's discussions, which I had already tried to analyse. However I realised that Anne would be much more likely to comment on individuals' quirks and how they were trying to manipulate each other. Thinking of Anne made me realise that I could see a whole set of categories for my data around the notion of motivations. I thought that Ben would be alarmed at my lack of data on how the team members looked and their tones of voice that reminded me to think about the interpersonal dynamics of the group I had studied.

Why you might want to do it.

This technique can help you to see things in your data which you would otherwise miss. It can also help you to get an idea of how others may react to your findings, which will help you in presenting your work to others later. It costs nothing to do and you can spend just as long on it as seems productive to you.

It may help to talk out loud 'in role', but beware of eavesdroppers!

How to do it.

Pick specific people, rather than whole classes of individuals. Write down their names, try to recall their appearance and bring to mind their interests and characters.

Then role play it: pretend that they have come to see you and say out loud something like: 'Ah, hello Jo. How are your rabbits coming along? And are you still going to that women's group? Look, I've got this transcript of a conversation that I had last week with one of my group and I think you'd find it interesting because...' Pretend that you are telling Jo to her face what is interesting about this transcript.

Then switch roles and pretend to be Jo reading some of the data. If you can remember how she speaks, read bits of it aloud 'in role'. Stop every half page or so to think how Jo would be reacting to what she is reading, and try to express that out loud using her kind of phrasing.

This probably sounds very difficult to do but I have found that it works well for me. It may help to try to imagine a discussion with your imaginary friend. Ask her questions such as those below and try to guess how she would answer:

* Well, what do you think of that then?

* Does that remind you of anything?

* Are you surprised they said that?

* What interests you in that?

Note down anything interesting that this process reveals and then move on to another role.

18 Annotating the record

Example.

You are reading through your notes from observing classroom interactions. Half-way down the page, you realise that at this point the children on the right hand side of the room were all looking out of the window. You add this thought. After reading another paragraph, you are reminded by your data of a reference that you meant to read, and you add 'See Bloggs ref.' When you get to the bottom of the page, you have a sense that the last few interactions may have been all about control, so you note that too.

Why you might want to do it.

This technique helps you to avoid losing any possibly helpful thoughts, without developing a separate second set of materials. However, you may find that the original data gets too full with all these annotations.

How to do it.

You want to catch all the thoughts that you have while reading your data. You may have some of the following.

* Additions to your observations that you omitted to note before.

* Ideas about common points, categories or emerging generalisations.

* Reactions of surprise or recognition.

* Cross references to other related data.

* Anything else that you do not want to forget.

You may be able to add some of these thoughts while making your original written or taped record. If your notes or transcripts are already completed, then you need a way of inserting these later thoughts into the record. The simplest way is to keep written records on one side of the paper only, leaving the backs of the sheets for these annotations. If you prefer to write between the lines or in the margins, you probably ought to make a photocopy of the original data first. If your data is on a word processor, it is easy to insert extra text wherever you want it.

You will need a convention to show that these are your annotations and not part of the original record. Look at Item 10: *Adding your own comments* for some suggestions. You can save both original and annotated versions as separate files. This way you need never lose access to a clean original.

If you want to add more annotations at subsequent readings of your data, then you can do so. It can help to date all these additions.

How to recognise and pattern your own ideas about your data

How to recognise and pattern your own ideas about your data

What are you trying to do?

After you have studied your data carefully and immersed yourself in it, you need to step back and think about it. This is the task that takes you beyond description of your data to interpretation. You are trying to discover the significance of your findings, to see what they add to existing knowledge. For some studies, this stage may not be necessary at all. If description is sufficient, or you are only doing the research in order to check something, you may not need to develop an interpretation.

It is important to understand the inherent limitations on interpretations of qualitative data. There are two key points. The first is that you can only offer a personal interpretation and other interpretations will always be possible. Meaning is personal and events have different meanings for those present, for you and for your clients. Meanings can also change with time.

The second key point is that you have made a limited case study and you cannot be sure how far your interpretation applies outside that case study. You may want to suggest that your interpretation might apply more widely. In that case you need to be clear that you are only suggesting hypotheses that might be worth exploring in these wider settings, no more.

What is this going to be like?

Many researchers find it very hard to stop collecting and describing data: they are reluctant to turn to interpreting it. You are probably aware that the methodological literature is very firm about the importance of looking out for concepts and patterns throughout the time of collecting data, so that you can progressively focus on the most significant informants or situations. However, in practice it is quite rare to do much serious interpretation before you have stopped collecting data. This may be forced on you by practical constraints of time and opportunity to be in the field. For many researchers it is probably more a result of their reluctance to begin interpretation.

You may feel, modestly, that you cannot begin to interpret a small amount of data even having read Item 16: *Concentrating on a single instance*. If this is your first experience of qualitative research, you may suffer from culture shock and lack confidence in the rules of this new game. For some there is safety in the relatively routine procedures of collecting, coding and categorising data. Reading or listening to your own data can also be interesting and undemanding.

However, discovering your own ideas about your data is also the most interesting part of the work. It is the truly creative stage, the most exciting and satisfying part of being a researcher. You will have sudden flashes of inspiration and days when concepts form and you feel that it is all nearly in your grasp.

It is very common to feel worried by the uncertainty of this part of analysis. Most successful qualitative researchers have gone through times when they felt that they would never be able to reach a usable interpretation of their findings. They feel that they have only a heap of disconnected observations; they cannot find the story behind the words; they cannot see the picture as a whole. They may have lists and lists of categories but no model of how these are inter-related. Or they may feel that there are innumerable possible interpretations, that any pattern is feasible and that there is no way of deciding between them.

You may feel at this stage that you are just not clever enough to do this kind of research. At the same time you may believe that most published studies have had their data doctored to support their interpretations!

So, how can you cope?

It will probably help to remind yourself of those limitations mentioned above: that meaning is personal and that your interpretation is based on a small sample.

The essential strategies are **playing with ideas** and **using others.**

Playing with ideas is an attitude to your work that allows you to be creative. It can involve drawing or trying role-playing. It is better to approach both these experiments with an open mind and abandoning them if they do not feel right. It means that you no longer try to rely on set procedures or hard work. You allow yourself to have confidence in your own abilities and you enjoy the analysis.

Using others is a powerful strategy for externalising your own ideas. The idea is not so much that other people will have good ideas about your research, but rather that in talking about your work to them you will develop and clarify your own thinking. As usual in this work, you will also need to select techniques that suit you and your study.

Summary

Aims	- Discover the significance on your findings. - Find a personal interpretation. - Develop hypotheses applicable beyond your case-study.
Feelings	Worried about your ability to find any interpretations. Worried that you may be unable to choose from many possible interpretations. Scepticism about other studies, Joy in your creativity. Excitement at making an original contribution to knowledge.
Strategies	Playing with ideas. Using others. Select techniques.
Techniques	Sentence completions. Self-interrogation. Hypothetical questions. Brainstorming. The researcher's diary. Letters to friends. Conversations. Multiple reports. Seminars. Visualising your audience. Outlining your report. Mini-papers. Drawing pictures. Missing categories. Scatter diagram. Borrowing theories. Geometrical shapes.

19   Sentence completions

Example.

I had a supervisor for my doctoral research who was very good at asking helpful questions. I took him some material about a meeting which I was finding it hard to interpret. He asked me apparently obvious questions like 'What do you feel is significant about this meeting?' and 'How did it differ from other meetings?'.

After a few supervisions like this, I found that I could anticipate his questions and became able to make statements about my material without his prompting. I could invent my own incomplete sentences and use them to develop my ideas.

On one sheet of paper I wrote the following starter and found three ways of completing it.

```
I think the significant thing about this meeting is ...
    it was when the team identified an outside 'enemy'
    they started using the language of 'them and us'
    they seemed to settle down as a group who really
    liked each other
```

On a second sheet of paper I wrote the following new starter and found four ways of completing it.

```
This meeting was different from the others in that ...
    no-one remarked on my presence
    it was held off-campus
    the BBC member was not present
    we had the first draft of the unit to look at.
```

Why you might want to do it.

This technique can be very profitable, producing a string of new and powerful summarising ideas.

How to do it.

You can invent your own sentences or try some of the following.

* This section of data is all about...

* What I think is odd about this is...

* The main things that I want to say about this informant are...

* The really interesting thing about all this is that...

Write your incomplete sentences down, each at the top of a new sheet of paper. Try to write as many different completions to the sentence as possible in five minutes, then move on to the next sheet. If you run out of ideas before the five minutes is up, say the incomplete sentence aloud, over and over again, and a new ending may come to you.

Then take some time to study what you have written, to see what ideas there are in your completions of these sentences.

You can use this technique at any level of detail: on a few pages of data, about a set of observations, or about your data as a whole.

If you find that you cannot answer your own questions at first, try some of the other tips in this section for a while and then return to this approach.

20   Self-interrogation

Example.

In studying induction systems for professionals who make a mid-career switch, you have a vague idea that some of your informants have difficulty when they have to join an established team. By asking yourself the following questions, you might be able to develop a concept of 'the new member'.

* Why do I believe they have this problem?
* How do they show that they are in difficulty?
* Is it the same problem for all of them?

Why you might want to do it.

Self-interrogation often reveals more about your own ideas. You may feel that you have no basis for these early ideas, but I often find that I can dredge up all sorts of bits of evidence to defend myself when faced with specific questions. Exploring such critical questions also prepares you for real debates about your work.

Like all the tips for exploring your ideas, you might be tempted to spend too long on this technique. Only you can judge what would be sensible and which ideas to explore.

How to do it.

You can invent your own questions, or try some of the following.

* What is my evidence for that?

* What do I really mean by that?

* How can I reject the alternatives?

You could try to imagine that you are a critic of your own work: perhaps an examiner, a rival consultant, or tough colleagues in a seminar. Imagine that your work belongs to someone else and then role play a critic, being as hard on it as possible. Then go back to being yourself and try really hard to defend your ideas, as though they were part of your final well-prepared analysis. It can help to ask the questions out loud and then try to answer them in detail, as though face to face with your critic. After a few minutes stop and jot down the points that you have heard yourself make in defending your work. When you have used several questions in this way look at these jottings and try to see what new points are there.

You can use this approach at any level of detail: on a few pages of data, about a set of observations, or about some of your emerging ideas about all your data, taken as a whole. Obviously, you do not want to try it on all your ideas. Select those that seem important but ill-defined.

21   Hypothetical questions

Example.

After observing physiotherapists at work, I asked myself the following questions:

*   What would X have done if the patient had refused to listen to her advice?
*   What would she have done if the physician had said Y?
*   What would she have done if the patient had failed to return for his next appointment?

Why you might want to do it.

Using hypothetical questions can round out your initial ideas. If you can answer such questions readily, it shows how well you understand your data and that is good for your confidence.

However, if you find that you cannot speculate in this way, remember that the reason may be that this technique does not suit you, or that you need to spend more time absorbing the data you already have. It does not mean you need to go out and ask all these questions in the field.

How to do it.

The first thing you need are some ideas of questions that might reveal more about your characters or situations. You might be able to develop them by completing sentences such as the following.

*   What would they have said if...

*   What would they have done if...

*   What would have happened if...

*   What stopped her from...

*   Why didn't they...

You may be able to think through your own answers to these questions straight away. It can help ideas to flow if you imagine that each of your informants in turn is sitting in front of you. Ask them your hypothetical questions out loud and answer them yourself, pretending to be each of your informants in turn. Jot down the points that you have made in your answers as you go along. Occasionally it may be necessary to return to your informant but remember that you are trying to explore your own thinking about the data that you already have.

It is the points that you make in answering your questions that need attention, to see what they reveal about your ideas.

22   Brainstorming

Example.

You are preparing a report on the encouragement of research in polytechnics. Within this you might want to develop your ideas about the different methods that you have discovered are being used in supervising research students. You could write down a question such as:

How **could** people supervise research students?

In answering it you might include all sorts of ideas, such as:

By working with them on a joint task.

By telephone.

By asking them to make written reports.

By arranging for them to meet significant people.

By putting them in pairs.

When you look at these ideas, you might find that three of them you had already identified as being used by the supervisors of your sample of informants. However, you might also realise that your data suggests that the students are being asked to meet other research workers in their field, by being invited to faculty seminars. This gives you a fourth possible method to explore. The fifth idea, of putting them in pairs, might not seem to be being used and you can either discard it or note it for use when you come to think about possible changes that should be made in supervision practices.

Why you might want to do it.

Brainstorming can be fun, especially if you can do it in a group. Sometimes it can lead to new insights into your material. However, it will not work unless you can let go and play with ideas, which may mean working in an unfamiliar way. You have to convince yourself that, in this context, play is work.

How to do it.

The essence of the approach is to play with ideas: to get out of your analytical, evaluative frame of mind and to feel that 'anything goes'.

Begin by forming a question. You can either make it a question about what your data show, or more hypothetically, as I did in the example above, a question about what could happen in the kind of situations that you are studying. You want a question that calls for specific answers. Write your question out at the top of a sheet of paper.

Then try to answer it in as many different ways as possible. At this stage there is no need to elaborate each answer, just list them by jotting down a few words to help you remember them later. You want as many ideas as possible and are not concerned about their quality. Try not to let yourself comment mentally on each idea. Some may seem little different from an earlier idea in your list. Some may seem quite useless or silly, but do not censor them at this stage.

The last step, when you seem to have run out of ideas, is to look at your list carefully. Think which of these ideas you had already identified as being shown by your data. Are any of the others also implied, although not expressed in quite the same way? Is it odd that others on your list have not been revealed in your data?

This is not traditional brainstorming, which is a group technique for generating a wide range of ideas to solve a problem. However, if you can get friends to join you, it can be useful and enjoyable. Write the starter question up where you can all see it. Take five minutes silence first, in which everyone jots down as many ideas as possible on a bit of paper. Then take it in turns to read out just one idea each. After a while, when people start to run out of their written ideas, they may find that other ideas occur, provoked by what they are hearing from others in the group. The essential rule in a group is that no-one may criticise, even jokingly.

23   The researcher's diary

Example.

Here are a few excerpts from the research diary that I kept when I was studying how Open University academics drafted correspondence lessons.

15th Aug. 1977
I have been trying to categorise data and I can't
do it. I have no confidence in my categories. . .
I have forced myself to mock-up a set of chapters
as a record of my silly state of thinking, 30
pages, but I have not shown them to anyone.

July 1978
I have tried to get (3 informants) to make taped
diaries for me while they are drafting, with lousy
results. They find it difficult and can't do it
while writing, only retrospectively. Several of
the tapes are unintelligible: batteries running
out, held mic too close to mouth, a heavy cold.

6th Aug. 1979
I sent (supervisor) the 2 chapters on writing. He
suggested alternative sub-headings but stressed
that Ed. Tech. separates decisions on curriculum
from their implementation and wants me to show how
decisions on concept contents change during
development. He liked my phrase 'finding words'.

17th Aug. 1979
Talking to (friend). Dominant themes emerging from
my case study are: designing and implementing are
integrated; strong urge to find a coherent unique
pattern; the 'audience' is multiple and shifting;
(its a fearful, communally taboo area); (choice of
words is still hard even after a tight plan).

Why you might want to do it.

The main intention in keeping a diary is to bring out your ideas into the open. By forcing you to review them and record them, you will inevitably develop them. You will discover things about your data that you did not know you knew.

A diary can help you emotionally, as well as helping you to recognise your own ideas. You can be honest in your diary and that helps to relieve your feelings. By reading over your diary you will probably get a sense of progress. Things that were problems a few weeks ago have often resolved themselves or no longer seem so significant.

A diary can be helpful if you have to write up your research methods, especially if you believe that your feelings have influenced your data. In some forms of qualitative research you may be asked to include such a diary in your final report. In that case your diary may need only a little editing to provide what you need.

However, not everyone finds it easy to write freely in a diary format and you may decide that this is too introspective for you. Other researchers enjoy this kind of personal writing to such an extent that they write what amounts to novels about the lives of qualitative researchers. While some of us would like to read such novels, writing one might distract you from the research that you had in mind.

How to do it.

Have a notebook for the diary so that you can carry it around, or a file for entries made on odd scraps of paper.

Try to make a few notes on five different sorts of items:

*   Your feelings about the work

*   Accounts of your methods, what you have done and how it worked out

*   Ideas, concepts, categories and hypotheses

*   What seems to be important

*   What you plan to do next

Try to write for yourself alone, as fully and honestly as you can. The diary is your confidante. If you want to use any of its entries later you can always copy them out in an edited form.
You can make records whenever you feel that something important has happened, or when you want to review your progress. If you find that you forget to record anything for several weeks it can help to think back and summarise nonetheless.

Read your diary over at intervals, especially when you feel that you are making no progress.

There are several books and articles in the form of researchers' diaries, which I find enjoyable reading. You might like to try Bell and Encel, 1978. Hockey, 1985 intersperses advice to researchers on nursing with her own experience as a researcher.

References

Colin Bell & Solomon Encel (eds) *Inside the Whale: ten personal accounts of social research*,
                                   Pergamon Press, 1978.
Lizbeth Hockey   *Nursing Research*
                                   Longmans, 1985.

24   Letters to friends

Example.

I used to imagine that I was writing to my sister Carol.

>   Milton Keynes
>   Monday
>
> Dear Carol,
> Sorry I haven't written for such ages but I've
> been pretty busy and this research project is
> really getting me down. I don't know why I
> ever started it!
>
> The main problem is I've got so much data –
> forty three files, would you believe! I'm
> sure most of it can be safely binned but I
> daren't do that at this stage. Actually I do
> find it fascinating to read through. I'm
> tempted just to dump the lot on Dr. P. and
> tell him its all in there and I'd be doing it
> an injustice if I attempted to summarise
> life's rich pattern.
>
> Maybe I'll find a neat story to tell him soon,
> there do seem to be some interesting bits
> around ideas like negotiation and motivations,
> but I haven't got enough categories to look
> academically respectable yet.
>
> Yours, in semi-despair,
>
>   *Judith* x

Why you might want to do it.

The letter format makes you boil your thoughts down to a few pithy sentences and this summarising can focus your mind on the many interesting elements in your findings. Writing in an informal style can help you to distance yourself and to see your ideas afresh. You may find that you are more willing to speculate in this informal format and that you write about ideas which are only just beginning to form and which you would not consider mentioning to your colleagues.

Recording positive comments about your work can be cheering. Alternatively, it can be a relief to confess how much you are hating the work.

You can scribble a letter like this in odd moments and it can be quite amusing to try. However, you may feel rather silly and find it difficult to get into the right mood. The technique only works as well as you can suspend disbelief and play along with the pretence.

How to do it.

To make this suggestion work, you have to convince yourself that you really are writing a letter to a real person. Choose someone to whom you do write informal letters. Use the kind of paper and pen that you normally use for letters. Put your address at the top and the date. Start with a friendly sentence that is nothing to do with your research, to get in the mood.

Then write about your research. Try not to slip into formal academic language, or into referring to theories or references. Use slang, exclamation marks, abbreviations, exaggeration or whatever style is appropriate for the friend that you have in mind. If you get stuck, you could try Item 19: *Sentence completions* but turn them into informal language. You might try:

* I suppose the real reason I started this project was...

* I'm quite excited as it seems I may have discovered that...

* I'm just guessing but it almost seems as if ...

You might refer to any comments that have been made about your work and how you are feeling about it at present. Read it through to see what you have said that is new.

Of course, you are really looking for a 'confidante', and if you have a close but <u>non-involved</u> friend who might be interested, you could write and send real letters. Remember to file a copy of it away in your researcher's diary as decribed in Item 23.

25   Conversations

Example.

I find it helpful to talk to interested friends about my latest ideas about the meaning of my data. In one case I talked about my project on social workers dealing with child abuse with another researcher who is using repertory grids to do some psychology research and who I meet every couple of months. It's helpful for me to explain what I've done since we last met and why - in this case that I have made three trips to watch court proceedings - and how this differed from what I had intended to do.

Why you might want to do it.

Contrary to what you might think, most people are pleased to be used in this way and will find your work interesting. Qualitative research is nearly always full of human interest and originality.

The struggle to express yourself simply seems to have enormous value. You may see your work in a new way, a gaping hole in the argument may be revealed, even though you have gone through your ideas on paper many times. In giving continuity to your conversation you may find that you have linked ideas in a new way, or described a new group of ideas that can now be elaborated.

As opposed to almost all my other suggestions, I do not think you can spend too much time talking about your work. It is difficult if you are shy, or particularly uncertain of your ground, but it is worth trying to overcome your fears and inhibitions. Talking through the evidence, trying to develop an argument, checking out tentative ideas with another, are all powerful ways of developing a deep approach to the processing of information which underpins success in other areas of study.

How to do it.

The principle that you must follow is to ACCEPT ALL POSSIBILITIES OF TALKING ABOUT YOUR WORK. Do not exclude complete lay-people: in trying to interest them and to explain things without using specialised terminology your may catch yourself using some very neat simplifying ideas. If someone asks what you are doing these days, tell them. If a friend remarks on your pallor, explain it. If a colleague enquires how the work is going, describe your progress. If no-one asks you anything, invite yourself into conversations. This is no time to worry about boring people and you can end by thanking them and apologising for making use of them in this way. When the conversation is over, try to note any new insights and capture any neat turns of phrase that you used.

You will need to be aware of possible breaches of confidentiality in discussing your data with others. Be rigorous with yourself. Stick to principles and procedures and only use general or anonymous examples. Do not reveal the thoughts and feelings of your subjects which have been offered to you in confidence.

26   Multiple reports

Example

You are studying clients' reactions to certain Social Services for a written report to members of a District Health Authority. You draw up rough plans for a practical article in the Health Service Journal and a more theoretical article for the *British Journal of Sociology*. You also work out the bones of talks that you could give to the relevant local voluntary society, to colleagues in your department at work and to a group of Health Education tutors who invite you to their seminars. You also design a plan for further research on your topic.

Why you might want to do it.

This technique will help you to sort out your ideas about your data. It will help you to see which ideas belong in your final report and which, although equally fascinating, need to be omitted. Having outlined other products that might flow from the research, you may feel more able to put them aside and focus on the immediate task of getting out your report. In beginning to envisage that final report you may find that your ideas become clearer and begin to take on a more recognisable structure.

However, be wary of becoming sidetracked and allowing yourself to spend too long detailing any of these other outlets. Equally, you do not want to become daunted by a sense of having to prepare a too large a series of events and documents.

How to do it.

Make a list of all the different ways in which your research might be expressed to an audience. This is not a realistic list, you may well not use any of these outlets but you can usefully explore what might go into each. Include both publications and spoken occasions. Include your main report for the research. Take a separate sheet of paper for each possible outlet and head it with a one line title which conveys the format and the content. So, in the example above, one sheet would be headed: 'Talk to Eastminster Voluntary Society'.

Then make some sort of plan for each outlet, writing about a page for each. You need to write enough for the outlet to become real to you, so that you can envisage it as a finished product. To help you do this you might rough out its audience or readership, give an estimate of its duration or length, and note any ideas for illustrations, as well as indicating the contents list.

27   Seminars

Example.

You are leading a seminar for a group of other researchers who are all interested in qualitative research. You tell them briefly why you had embarked on your research project and outline your methods. Then you give them copies of a single page of a transcript of a discussion among your informants, to illustrate your findings. You spend the bulk of your allotted half hour on your first ideas about what it all means and mention the ideas that you have already abandoned. You criticise the ideas that you are still holding. When you finish, your audience asks questions and make suggestions. With any luck you will suddenly be able to see far more possibilities in your illustrative page of transcript. You may see links to many different kinds of existing concepts and theories. You will probably also see further limitations in your own ideas.

Why might you want to do it.

Preparing for a seminar is very helpful in sorting out your ideas. Your audience will probably be able to give you a sense of weaknesses and strengths in your work and new ideas to follow up.

However, you do run the risk of being discouraged by a group who are not feeling helpful. Some seminar groups have a tradition of point-scoring behaviour. If the idea of a seminar is very frightening, it may not be worth the risk. To be useful, you will probably need to give the idea at least 2 or 3 days of preparation. If you are worried about it, it will distract you from other work until it is over. You may have travel expenses or photocopying costs.

How to do it.

The first problem may be to find a seminar audience. If you are based in an academic institution that is unlikely to be difficult. Ask lecturers and research students in your own or other related departments. If you are not based in a college it is still worth considering this technique. Most institutions of higher education run a regular seminar series and are willing to organise a one-off occasion, especially if you offer to talk about your work without a fee. Work in progress is often more illuminating for students than the more common offers of talks about completed and polished research. Another possibility is to offer your 'seminar' as a conference contribution. Look for conferences on related fields or on qualitative research and see if they have 'workshop' sessions, as these will give you lots of time for the feedback that you want. Even if it has to be a formal 'paper', you will probably find that some conference participants will be keen to discuss your work between the presentations.

Plan your seminar so that you ALLOW AT LEAST HALF YOUR ALLOTTED TIME FOR QUESTIONS AND SUGGESTIONS. If you have not given a seminar before, get some ideas for structuring it from, for example Habeshaw S et al, 1989. Make some notes and take a small piece of your data to show. It helps to do a practice run of what you intend to say and do, partly to give you confidence on the day and partly to check that your plan is not overambitious for the time available.

Then your main concern is to work out what you want from your audience and how to persuade them to give you this. It usually helps if you are quite open about what you want. You may want them to:

*   React with alternative interpretations

*   Help you to see links between different parts of your ideas

*   Expose the assumptions which underlie your thinking

*   Give you contacts and references to find others in your field

Reference

Habeshaw S et al   *53 Interesting Things to do in Your Seminars and Tutorials*,
                          Technical and Educational Services, Bristol, 1989, 3rd Edn

28   Visualising your audience

Example.

When I was doing research on how people drafted reports, I worked out that the potential audiences for this work would include:

*   Colleagues at work who found it difficult to write

*   Qualitative researchers who would be interested in my methods

*   Cognitive psychologists who saw writing processes as their field.

Taking the example of the cognitive psychologists, I decided that they would expect to find reference to their body of theory and a thorough knowledge of it. They would love to find something that elaborated their theories, without denying their basic paradigm. They would feel comfortable if I included some quantitative experimental data. If they read my report their assumptions would include the following:

-    That the productive approach for studying writing is to make models of an individual's mental process

-    That there is no need for these models to be based on studies of actual writing behaviours in real-life situations

-    That the process of writing is best described as a series of interacting mental processes, which refine and clarify the author's intentions

-    That the writing occurs at a single sitting.

Why you might want to do it.

This technique may throw up new ways of looking at your ideas and it can help in other ways too. It can be a quick way of getting a sense of reality about finishing a long project. It should help you to get a perspective about the importance of your findings. It should help you to plan your final report: you will see better what will need careful explanation and what to emphasise. You may also see new markets for your work.

Despite these spin-off benefits you can easily spend an unjustified amount of time on this technique. However, its greatest danger is probably that it can be depressing. You may realise that one of your major audiences is going to be inherently hostile to your approach, as I did in the example above. You may see that in order to satisfy them you will have to tackle whole additional literatures. My advice then is to think hard and then think again and be very wary of trying to accommodate everyone.

How to do it.

List each potential audience on a separate sheet of paper and then try to describe their likely views on your work. You might try answering such questions as:

* What are their expectations likely to be of your findings?

* What would they love and hate to find in your work?

* What are their existing views about your topic?

* What are the assumptions behind their ideas?

* What is their theoretical stance, paradigm or ideology?

* What are their practical concerns?

If you find that you cannot answer such questions about an important audience, it is probably worth finding a representative of that group to interview briefly.

When you have the answers to your questions, look to see if they suggest new ways of looking at your ideas about your data, or new ways of organising your existing ideas.

29   Outlining your report

Example.

When carrying out a 2 year project on ward supervision of learners I had gathered preliminary data for 2 months. At this point I sat down and jotted a rough contents list.

```
Introduction to the topic         2 pages
Justification of the research     5 pages
Ch. 1:  characters and actors     5 pages
Ch. 2:  stages in the play        2 pages
Ch. 3:  types of responses       10 pages
Conclusions                       5 pages
```

Why you might want to do it.

It can be very encouraging to envisage your final report; it can give you a sense that the analysis will have an end. But the main aim is to help you to externalise your ideas, to envisage alternative ways of grouping and sequencing your thoughts, and to sum up your half-formed ideas by having to name them. Estimating the length of sections should help to develop your sense of the relative importance and difficulty of your ideas.

How to do it.

You can try this technique several times during your analysis, remembering each time that it is an aid to thinking, and does not determine what your real final report will look like. You can do it knowing that you are still going to collect more data, or that when you have looked more carefully at your findings you will almost certainly change some of these ideas.

You might try a contents list with an estimate of page numbers, as in the example above. Or you might draft sections in note form. If you try a contents list, start by noting 'introduction' and 'conclusion'. Then divide up your ideas into a few chunks. Think of a name for each chunk and label them as numbered chapters. Will you need any other sections, such as appendices or a separate methods chapter? In estimating the length of each chapter, you are only trying to get a rough idea of their relative sizes.

30   Mini-papers

Example.

You are doing research on relationships between schools and their pupils' homes as part of a degree in Education. Your supervisor spots that you are feeling reluctant to begin analysis at all and persuades you to write two short pieces. One is an account of a parent-teacher meeting and one a description of how one teacher had reacted to a parent's request. Each paper that you write is just a few pages and takes up to half a day to write. In discussing them with your supervisor you see that you felt that there was a lot that had been hidden and not said openly at the parent-teacher meeting and that the teacher reacted to the parent's request in the light of that hidden knowledge.

What you might want do about it.

In writing you will probably find that you have more ideas than you thought you had. Writing down the obvious points, as well as the more tentative interpretations, usually makes quite a long list of ideas. You may also gain by studying what you have written: seeing the relationships between ideas. Writing some short pieces is also good practice for your final report and may prevent the 'writing block' that is so common in research. You should treat these short pieces as part-drafts of the final version and not as the finished product. However, IT IS DANGEROUS TO FEEL THAT YOU CANNOT BEGIN TO WRITE UNTIL YOU HAVE COLLECTED AND ANALYSED ALL YOUR DATA.

How to do it.

Choose a very small circumscribed topic, such as a particular data collection occasion, or a single type of behaviour, function, problem or motivation. Make notes on what you can say about this topic at this stage in your analysis. You can use such phrases as:

*   From the data I have it looks as if ...

*   There could be ...

*   I guess that ...

*   One way to look at this is to see it as ...

* Some of the categories might be ...

If you can arrange to discuss your notes with someone, that will probably enhance the nature of the exercise. Whether alone or in discussion ask yourself questions such as:

* Have I made all the obvious points, as well as mentioning my original ideas?

* What have I said that I would not have said before I began this research?

* How does this material relate to my idea of my final report?

You can use this technique at any stage in the analysis but it is probably most useful early on, long before you would normally expect to start drafting anything.

31   Drawing pictures

Example.

I once had an idea that a very successful lecturer whom I had studied was effective for two main reasons. The first was that he knew his students: what they already knew about his subject, what they would find difficult about the new material and how fast they could absorb new ideas. Secondly, he knew his material and he knew what he felt would be of value in it for his students.

I realised that I saw this as a picture, with the lecturer as an engineer at a drawing board. He was designing a route for a railway line, through mountainous scenery. My analogy was that the students were trains, who had to be conducted safely through the subject mountains, at an appropriate gradient.

Why you might want to do it.

The aim is to catch some of the essence of your ideas by using this unusual summarising device. Drawing can help you to see your ideas afresh and by association may provoke new ideas too. It can be a pleasant way to play with your ideas.

You may feel quite incapable of drawing anything, the very idea makes you dry up! However, you may be able to visualise your ideas as images. Drawing ability doesn't matter: these representations are for your eyes only and IT DOESN'T MATTER IF YOUR SKETCH WOULD LOOK SCRAPPY OR MEANINGLESS TO ANYONE ELSE.

How to do it.

Take a group of your ideas that seem to go together. Ask yourself:

* If I had to draw a cartoon to illustrate them, what would it look like?

* How could I express them in a diagram?

* How would an artist represent them? Is there, for example, a particular character doing something, or a particular situation that he could use to illustrate your ideas?

Sketch out one or more of these approaches. Pretend you're back in Primary School and use fat felt tip pens in various colours if they are available, remembering that you need never show the results to anyone!

You may like to follow this up by telling other people about your visual analogy or model, to help you to discover what this technique has done for your interpretation.

32   Missing categories

Example.

In studying how new mothers coped with the first few weeks of looking after their babies, you find that you have collected a lot of data on what you call 'feeding problems'. You also have details of how the mothers coped with feeding under the heading of 'tactics'. You have noted various problems with their babies' sleeping habits. When you consciously look for missing categories, you spot that you had not thought about 'sleeping tactics'.

Why you might want to do it.

This approach to elaborating your material can be quite fruitful and can be used several times over. It costs nothing except a little time. However, avoid any temptation to invent data that you have not actually collected in the field, or to adjust your findings to make them look better.

How to do it.

Some missing categories may be obvious, as in the example above. You may be able to find more by using questions such as the following.

* Could I elaborate any group usefully by sub-dividing it?

* Do any of these categories have opposites?

* Are there any implications that follow from these behaviours?

* Are there categories of causes that I could add?

* Can any of these groups of categories be linked into a cycle or a sequence by adding a few more categories?

It may be easiest to see missing categories if you have represented the relationships between your ideas visually, using a matrix or network as in Items 33:*Scatter diagram* and 35: *Geometrical shapes*.

33   Scatter diagram

Example.

You are trying to analyse ideas about how students write essays and project reports. The whole scatter diagram would be too big to reproduce here but one corner of your first attempt looks like this:

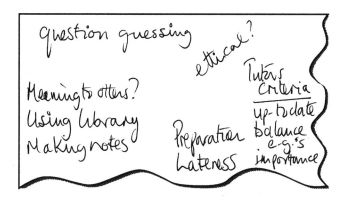

After some thought you see ways of reorganising it and tidy it up into the version shown below.

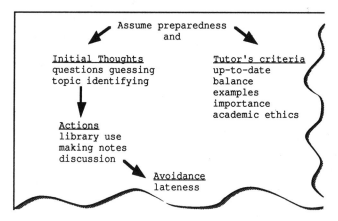

Why you might want to do it.

This technique may begin to show you that your mass of apparently undifferentiated ideas has some structure in your mind: possible patterns for your story may start to emerge. It can also help you to sum up the essence of your ideas by forcing you to find short names for each category. It can help you to see that you have more ideas than you had thought and it can of itself provoke you to add new categories.

If the big diagram does not lead you to see any relationships, it could be discouraging. However, you will not have wasted much time or money on it and you may find that you will see patterns in the scatter later on. Do not throw it away, but leave it for a while and then try one of the tips for using other people to reveal more of your ideas.

How to do it.

Get a few really large sheets of paper. Sugar paper or the back of used flip chart paper is ideal.

Make a list of all the ideas, groups of categories and concepts that seem to be emerging from your analysis. Include all the odd or conflicting bits and pieces, even if they do not seem to fit the overall picture at this stage. Give each a brief name that reminds you what it is about. There is no need to spend long on this as you can always change their names later on.

The next step is to transfer all these names onto a big sheet of paper, putting them all over, using all the space. The aim is to represent the relationships between your ideas visually, using distance on the paper to represent intellectual distance between ideas. I find it easiest to write the names in but you might prefer to write each on a movable slip of paper. Put the first name you pick up near the middle of the sheet. For the second name, think whether it seems to have some kind of relationship to the first name. If it has, place it fairly near it on the sheet. If you feel that they are very different, but not a simple pair of opposites, add the second name far away from the first. Opposites could be in close parallel groups. Continue adding names from your list in this way until they are all somewhere on the big sheet.

Do not stop to move them around at this stage, even if you change your mind and feel a name is in the wrong position. You could add some arrows to catch these thoughts, as I did in the example shown above. Do not worry if you do not know where to put a name, just add it in any space, perhaps with a question mark to record your uncertainty. At this stage you just want to get them all down quickly.

Now look at this big sheet. You may see some tidying up that you could do, or that some names ought to be moved nearer or further from other groups of names. Look for groups that could now be given a group title. Draw lines between related groups and write the nature of the relationship along the line.

If you have written the names in, redraw the diagram more neatly, incorporating all the improvements that you want to make. If you have used loose slips of paper, fasten them down now in their improved positions. You may be able to see that some groups of names can be extended with more similar categories or some opposites.

It can help to pin this second version of the diagram up where you work. Then you can amend it as your ideas develop. You can take it down, or make a smaller version to show to other people. You could do the whole technique on a white board, but working on a big sheet of paper encourages me to keep the diagram and return to it at intervals.

34   Borrowing theories

Example.

You are studying how managers deal with annual appraisal interviews. You happen to read *Developing Courses for Students* by Derek Rowntree and notice a section describing the idea of a 'spiral sequence': revisiting topics at different levels when learning complex inter-related ideas. (This idea was first described as the 'spiral curriculum' by Jerome Bruner in *The Process of Education*, 1961.) You consider this idea with its notions of circling round, revisiting and improving and see that it fits your own observations of managers' behaviour. You organise your emerging interpretation around this pattern and find that it helps you to draw out what seems to be important in a memorable way.

Why you might want to do it.

This technique can be productive, in that playing with existing theoretical ideas helps you to develop your thinking about your own data, even if you do not find a transferable pattern. Exploring existing theories in the way that I have suggested may help you to tie your own research into the literature, which is probably essential if you are a student.

However, there are dangers. The technique is time-consuming and it requires considerable mental agility. You may feel that your findings can be expressed in so many different ways that you despair of ever settling on a final report. You may be tempted to modify your findings to make them fit neatly into an existing model, particularly if that model would appear novel in your own field.

How to do it.

While you know that in qualitative research you must attempt to suspend your knowledge of existing theories in order to see your own material without preconceptions, you will obviously check whether your material fits an existing theory in your own field. I am suggesting that you also use theories that have been developed about quite unconnected fields. What you are hoping is that an idea will leap out at you as a fruitful way of looking at your own material.

One way of encouraging the flow of these kind of happy discoveries is to look at a basic textbook in a subject other than your own but close enough for you to be able to understand it readily. So, for example, if you are a sociologist look at textbooks in psychology or government or management or human geography. Look at the contents page and index to find the names of the main theories and concepts that are covered and check out those that sound interesting.

Another way is to make yourself a list of different kinds of theory, for example:

*   Categories of people and situations

*   Types and functions of organisations

*   Chronological series

*   Cause and effect models

*   Life cycles

*   Growth stages

*   Actors and roles

*   Socialisation, norms, deviance, social control

*   Gatekeepers

*   Problems and strategies.

Try to tell the story of your findings in terms of the different theories, using an externalisation technique such as Items: 19 *Sentence completions*, 23 *The researcher's diary*, 24, *Letters to friends*, or 25, *Conversations*. So, for example, if you were relating theories about bureaucracy in organisations to the effectiveness of the ambulance service you might start Item 19 by completing the following two half sentences.

*   The main actors in my story are...

*   The role played by the first actor is...

The final step is to think about what you have learned from playing with these ideas from other fields. If any of the theories or concepts seemed to transfer to your material well, what are the problems involved? You will need to check how much of your material fits comfortably into this kind of interpretation. You might also consider whether the theory that you might borrow is at a suitable level: is it a descriptive theory, or does it help to explain your findings? In applying the borrowed theory, you may have altered it so much that it needs a new name for your context, as well as an acknowledgement of its original source.

References

Derek Rowntree   *Developing Courses for Students*
                            Harper and Row, 1981.
Jerome Bruner   *The Process of Education*
                            Harvard University Press, 1961.

35 Geometrical shapes

Example.

You are studying the variety of approaches that doctors make to the idea of 'resource management': a new system of keeping track of treatments and their costs. You have a set of descriptive categories for how they see this concept as follows.

* threat to relationship with patients
* opportunity for career advancement
* it's about information technology
* management structures will have to change
* it will lead to privatisation of the NHS
* relationships with all staff will change
* need to persuade nurses to co-operate

The first geometric shape that you try is to see that these ideas could be expressed as three lists under the following headings.

1 Resource management is a technical system.
2 It is about persuading people to work differently.
3 It has big professional implications.

Later you try a spiral shape and find that this leads you to see the three lists as a sequence of change in the attitudes of individual doctors. One side of the spiral has been annotated in the diagram that follows, showing the developing attitudes to money.

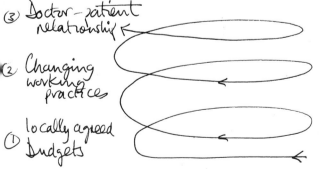

Why you might want to do it.

This technique can help you to consider alternative ways of expressing your findings, and help you to avoid fixing on the first pattern that comes to mind. It is quick to try and costs nothing. However, be wary of distorting your findings to make them a neater shape. If your data fall into a circular shape with a branch on the side, then that is what you have to retain.

How to do it.

Check out the fit to your data to a whole series of simple shapes. For example, do you seem to have elements of any of the following?

Lists, ordered sequences of items, or paired sequences?	
A range of dimensions or ranges, where your data can be seen as lying in straight lines between extreme values?	
Rectangles, usually a set of columns and rows, making up a matrix or table.	
Triangles, narrowing upwards from a broad base, or branching out upwards from a single point.	
Circles, like a life cycle or feedback circle.	

Overlapping circles,
like a Venn Diagram.

Spirals, like a repeating
circular pattern but each
time returning at a higher
level?

If any of these shapes seem promising, draw the shape boldly onto a large sheet of paper. Then write your categories onto the pattern. Remember that you might use combinations of shapes or different shapes for different parts of your findings.

Check out the value of such patterns for your data: either by discussing them with someone else or by asking yourself questions such as the following.

*   How much of your findings can be expressed in these shapes? Are some important parts of the data hidden?

*   Is the level of detail allowed by this pattern sufficiently elaborate?

*   Does it allow you to show the complexity of the relationships between the different parts of your findings?

How to organise evidence for your interpretation

How to organise evidence for your interpretation

What are you trying to do?

You need to convince yourself that the description and interpretation of your data is sound. If you are doing the research for a client, or as a student for a tutor or supervisor, you will also need to make a convincing case for your findings.

The essence of the task is to show that your data fit your story. At the very least, you need to be able to illustrate each point that you make with an example from your data. You will probably also want to make some kind of check for 'negative instances': data that seem to contradict your interpretation.

You may also want to show that you have considered other stories and that your data do not fit those interpretations as well.

What is this going to be like?

Some people enjoy this stage of a soft research project. Checking their ideas increases their sense of security and confidence. They like to know that they are on firm ground. Of course, if checking suggests that your interpretation does not fit the data particularly well.

Other people find this stage a chore, following on from the more exciting and creative work of forming an interpretation. It is a kind of 'housekeeping', like the early work on coding and filing your data.

So, how can you cope?

The essential strategies are to **assess your audience** and then **do the minimum**.

Textbooks on qualitative research, particularly the older ones, stress the importance of demonstrating evidence and they propose techniques which are very time-consuming. In reality, very few studies have devoted much effort to checking their interpretations. Studies which totally ignore the problem have been quite acceptable in many contexts. There are two useful questions to ask yourself about your clients, supervisor or yourself:

* How familiar are they with the soft qualitative approach to research?

* How exploratory is this research?

117

If you are doing the work for someone who is used to hard quantitative research and who will be very suspicious of your whole approach, then you have a problem. You will probably need to put a lot of effort both into justifying qualitative work in general (Item 45) and into providing evidence why they should accept your interpretation of the data. On the other hand, if you or your client are used to qualitative studies and are familiar with their conventions, then you may be able to omit this stage completely.

If your project is exploring a topic where little is known and few studies have already been done, then you have good justification for offering one possible interpretation. However, if you have studied a topic which others have looked at before, or where existing hypotheses would be expected to apply, then you will need to consider carefully how best to justify your own story of events.

Summary

Aims	- Convince that your story fits your data. - Show other stories fit less well. - Illustrate each point. - Show any negatives.
Feelings	Confident or dreadful, depending on the results. Bored by the chore.
Strategies	Assess your audience. Do the minimum.
Techniques	Use multiple sources. Using a second categoriser. Counting instances. Checking with informants. Relating your work to other studies. Using quotations. Adding quantitative data. Showing your credentials.

36   Using multiple sources

Example.

Your project team has been studying the management of time by executives in your organisation. You have decided to focus the interpretation of your findings around the concept of 'knowing what business we are in'. You could draw all your illustrations for the various categories of how people develop or avoid developing a clear sense of mission from a single interview with one department head who was passionate about this concept. Instead you choose three different sources of evidence.

* Quotations from seventeen different members of staff

* Quotations from a range of company documents

* Illustrations from directors' behaviour

Why you might want to do it.

You are probably already aware of the concept of 'triangulation', which is stressed in textbooks on qualitative research methods. Triangulation expresses the idea that you should collect your data in as many different ways and from as many different sources as possible. The hope is that the data from the different sources tells a similar story.

In using the full range of your data to illustrate your findings, you will offer a more convincing case than if you confine all your examples to just a few sources.

How to do it.

Make a list of all your informants and sources of data to see what the possibilities are. Distinguish different occasions, different settings and different methods used to record the data. When selecting quotations or illustrative points for your final report, check that you use as many of these different kinds of data as possible.

I often check which sources I have used after completing my report. I may note that three examples are not very clear and replace them with other quotations drawn from under-represented sections of my data. If I feel that too much of my evidence has been drawn from too few sources, I may add extra illustrations from other speakers, even if they are not such telling phrases.

You may want to consider returning to your informants to increase the usable evidence. Such 'progressive focussing', very acceptable in soft research, is exemplified in Item 11: *Returning for more data*. Ask yourself the following questions.

* Does my audience need a wide spread of evidence?

* Is there any doubt that the other sources will support my findings?

37   Using a second categoriser

Example.

You have transcripts of interviews with students about their opinions on learning and studying. You have developed various categories for describing their attitudes and techniques. You give a photo-copy of transcripts of four of the interviews to a friend and ask her to cut them up according to your categories. She takes an hour or two to do this and then you compare her little piles of paper with your own categorisation of that data. You find that she agreed with you over most of the categories but had interpreted one student's problems quite differently and had had difficulty in using your categories for student attitudes to being at college.

Why you might want to do it.

Preparing instructions for another person to use can help you to become much clearer about your categories and how you will describe them to others. It forces you to be explicit. Such assistants often come up with ideas that you have not considered before and which you can use to develop your interpretation. If you work with a partner and provide the same service for her work, you will get a chance to see another project at a similar stage, which can be very helpful.

However, she may not realise how much work you have already done to get this far and you will probably need to resist the temptation to pursue many new ideas at this stage. While this form of checking can be very helpful, you must remember that it has only checked categories and not your whole interpretation.

How to do it.

A good way of securing the services of a second categoriser is to offer to exchange: you will recategorise some of their data if they will do this job for you. Failing this, it is a job which could be done for money, paying by the hour. The best people to choose are those who understand something of the nature of qualitative data but who are not experts on your particular project topic.

The next decision is how much data to have reanalysed. Ideally you might want to have everything checked, but that would be very time-consuming. It might be sensible to try at first data that represents just a couple of hours of observations or discussions. Which sections of the data are likely to allow checking of most categories? Are there any sections of your data which it would be particularly helpful to have checked? If there are sections whose interpretation is crucial for your whole story about the data, or sections whose interpretation is doubtful and will be difficult to justify, then these are the ones to choose.

You need to provide your assistant with a clear written description of each category, probably a bit more than the key phrase by which you know it. For example, I had a category which I called 'private factors', which would not mean much to anyone else. I would have to explain that I meant those motivating factors which my informants would not normally express in public and that involved self-interest, such as seeking adulation, or avoiding work.

It is probably wise to tell them that you want them to read through all the data you have provided, before they start categorising. They also need to know whether they are allowed to give more than one category to a piece of data. They need to know how to record the categories that you choose. You might ask them to cut up a copy as in the example above. Alternatively you could develop line codes for your categories, as in Item 7, or number them in the margin.

After your assistant has completed her task, you need to compare her decisions with yours. You could do this by your overall impression, or count the numbers of instances which she categorises differently from you as a percentage of all the pieces of data. Counting is only worthwhile if your audience needs to know that you have made such a precise check. If there is less than about 70% agreement then you probably need to rethink your categories. Over about 70% agreement, it is still worth discussing the disagreements to see if you can improve your definitions of your categories, or if your own use of a category shifted over time. Often discussion of the discrepancies can increase agreement to about 90%. On the basis of such a degree of agreement you can be confident about the reliability of your categorisation.

When all this is over, do not forget to ask your assistant if they had any ideas about what your data signified!

38   Counting instances

Example.

In a study of students' attitudes to studying for a degree you have three categories for their attitudes to the reading that they do. The notes and transcripts have been categorised and cut up so that in your files for the reading categories there might be the following numbers of slips of paper:

Doing the minimum	3
Following instructions	11
Pursuing own interests	7

Why you might want to do it.

When you have completed your counts, you may use them to express your degree of confidence that your data really does support the points that you have called categories. Alternatively, you may use your tallies as an indication of how important or widespread each category is among your informants.

Counting instances is, however, time-consuming and tedious unless you have already got the data on a word processor or on punched cards (themselves time-consuming devices as explained in Items 4 and 5). If you do not have a clerk for this kind of work, you need to consider carefully whether it is really necessary. Many clients will happily accept an illustrative example of each of your categories and take their frequency of occurrence in your data on trust. If you are a student, it may be worth getting your tutor's advice on this point.

How to do it.

You need first to decide what counts as an instance of your category. It might be the number of informants mentioning something that is significant. If the same informant implies a similar point on another occasion, then you would not count that as another instance. However, you might wish to count the number of times a category came up in conversation with each informant, if that seems more significant.

If you have put your data on a word processor or punched cards, this is where those devices will come into their own. The word processor will almost certainly have a programme to enable it to find all instances of any word or phrase, which may be within the data or added by you as a marginal note. Using punched card needles, you can shake out all cards in a particular category and count them up.

If you have cut up the paper copies of your material according to categories, it is easy to count the number of slips of paper. Codes that are written in the margins of data are probably best counted by making yourself a table of categories before you start. Make a little mark for each instance and for the fifth mark put a line through the previous four, then start again with another little bunch, as shown below.

Category 1	IIIII IIIII IIII	=	14
Category 2	III	=	3
Category 3	IIIII II	=	7
Category 4	IIIII IIIII IIIII IIIII II	=	22

For some categories you may want to keep a separate tally of negative instances.

39   Checking with your informants

Example.

A colleague of mine was evaluating some Open University course materials by observing a group of students at their tutorials, while ostensibly taking the course herself. She found that most of the materials worked well and felt that she had a clear sense of the few changes that could improve the course. She went to one of the weekly student tutorial meetings and told them her views. She told them that she had not asked for their evaluation directly at first as she had not wanted them to feel like guinea pigs but rather had wanted to experience their and her reactions to studying in as normal a fashion as possible. They accepted this explanation, confirmed most of her evaluation and added two points of difficulty that individuals had not liked to mention in the previous tutorials.

Why you might want to do it.

If your informants broadly approve of your interpretation, at least you know that either it fits their perceptions of reality, or that it is a flattering interpretation which they do not find embarrassing! You may see this kind of checking as a way of democratising the process of research, of returning power to your informants. For example, many feminist researchers prefer to include any women that they study in a full participant relationship and see themselves as technicians helping those women to express their own views.

Be wary of giving your informants control over your interpretation case you end up with nothing that you are prepared to put your name to. Remember that you cannot rely on them to treat your preliminary findings as confidential. They could choose to tell the world their own version of your interpretation!

As with all forms of checking, you need to weigh the possible advantages and risks against the time it will take and whether such a check is expected by your audience.

How to do it.

Firstly, you need to decide if your informants will be able and willing to make this kind of check. If you share a common ground, such as a Sociology student studying other students, there should be few problems. It would be more difficult to use this technique if your informants were small children, or did not know that you were collecting data from them. If your data is about a complex social situation, then it may be that each informant will perceive what happened differently.

Remember that while soft research is generally interesting, many informants may be daunted by being offered a long document to read, or embarrassed to see all the incoherencies of their own speech on a transcript. They will be unlikely to want to debate the finer points of the differences between your categories. So you need to select what you show to your informants. It probably needs to be short and to avoid many direct quotations from their own speech. Summary descriptions of what you think went on in an encounter could be ideal. Interpretations that go beyond description may well be rejected by any participants who feel that you have shown them in a bad light. Giving them descriptions of other informants, rather than only material that relates directly to themselves, can help them to keep a sense of proportion.

You will need to explain how you are going to use the material that you give them, for example if it is going to be presented to anyone else, or is only for your eyes as the basis for further work. They may ask you how you are going to use their comments. You need to decide whether you are giving them any CONTROL over your final report, any power of VETO. Remember, if they dislike your interpretation, they might choose to break any CONFIDENTIALITY AGREEMENT that you have made and release some of your findings in a politically disastrous manner for you.

You need to be prepared to defend your choice of research method with some informants. I have found that repeated stress on the phrase 'exploratory case-study' defuses a lot of criticisms of unrepresentativeness.

40   Relating your work to other studies

Example.

You have made a study of the work of occupational therapists.

In your interpretation you focussed on the social relationship between the patient and the therapist. You have ideas about patients being able to identify with the therapists and about the importance of occupational therapists being seen as non-threatening, friendly people.

With the help of a librarian, you find about thirty possibly important publications. When you look at these, you find that they share a few key ideas about this job.

Occupational therapy is seen to be about:

* Treating the whole person
* Using the activities of daily life in treatment
* Developing abilities to function in daily life.

Your own interpretation can be seen as congruent with these key ideas, as drawing attention to something important that enables occupational therapists to work in the ways that the literature suggests.

Why you might want to do it.

If your study is in any kind of an academic context you will almost certainly be expected to 'review the literature'. If you can show that your findings support existing published hypotheses, then you can argue that that makes them more likely to be valid interpretations.

The ideal findings for a student would probably end up by developing existing ideas without actually challenging them! However, you may be open to criticism for having chosen too well-known an area for investigative qualitative research. Having an interpretation that is completely at odds with previous ideas about your area of study is equally difficult, for then you must expect more questioning of the reliability of your findings. In particular you need to be 100% sure that the data supports your interpretation? Above all, BE WARY OF CHANGING YOUR INTERPRETATION TO FIT EXISTING THEORIES. Quite apart from the ethics of this, you are likely to be caught because your data will not fit!

How to do it.

You need to start by identifying the existing ideas about your topic. If you are a student you may be able to refer to lecture notes or ask your supervisor for help. You may find a helpful librarian willing to conduct a literature search for you. Your library may have a computer programme which can search for you. Whether you have any of these resources or not, you need to make a list of what people believe about your topic, especially those to whom you will be presenting your findings. Item 28: *Visualising your audience* will help you with some ideas on how to do this.

Then ask yourself how your interpretation fits these theories and beliefs. Useful questions might include the following.

* Does my interpretation conflict with any of these ideas?

* Does it develop any of these ideas?

* Does it offer an explanation for any of these ideas?

* What would each of these ideas have predicted for my study?

41   Using quotations

Example.

In a study I made of people in meetings, I included how they reacted to reports that they wanted changed. I identified one of the tactics that they used as 'to minimise their own power': to make the author of the report feel that he is in charge and to stop him feeling threatened and defensive.

To illustrate this tactic in my report on my findings I quoted someone who began his comments to a report's author as follows.

> *I stand in a very awkward position because frankly I've had no time to read this properly or to comment on it in detail, but I'm wondering whether one couldn't...*

Not only did he declare himself to be in the wrong, but he also used a very tentative indirect style for his criticisms, which were in fact detailed and were accepted by the report's disarmed author.

Why you might want to do it.

Using quotations as a form of evidence is usually easy to do and very convincing. At least it shows that the whole thing is not entirely in your imagination! Readers enjoy the quotations and they break up what may otherwise be a turgid text.

Not all your points may be amenable to this way of providing evidence. The more subtle and complex concepts are most unlikely to be adequately illustrated by any one remark or observation. You might aim to use this technique only on your first order of points, your initial descriptive categories.

How to do it.

You are probably seeking only one or two quotations for each of your interpretative points. More than that gets too long to read.

Ideally you will have a pile of possible quotations ready, especially if you have some kind of filing system where your data has been categorised. Then you can just highlight and select one or two nicely expressed quotations. However, many of your points may not be developed until later in the analysis and may be more complex points than the simple initial categories. You may still be able to use your initial coding to help you find illustrative quotations for these complex points, assuming you can think of categories where the interpretative points are most likely to be made. If you are very familiar with your data, you may even remember a remark or an observation that illustrates your point. Then you have to hope your filing system is good enough for you to find that piece of data again.

Alternatively, you might be able to return to your informants and ask them a leading question which will produce a quotation that you can use. You have to be careful not to prompt the answer that you want too firmly. In the example above you might have asked a member of the meeting how she tried to help an author to accept her comments. You would not have asked directly if she ever tried to minimise her power, for that would tend to produce a simple 'Yes' or 'No' and not the convincing quotation that you need. You would also need to worry about her value as a witness if prompted too closely.

42   Adding quantitative data

Example.

You have made a study of six general practitioners which included an interpretation with a long list of the factors that you felt were motivating them. You check out this part of your interpretation by a survey of a much bigger sample of G.P.'s. You ask them to rate the importance to their own work of each of your factors. Tabulating their responses might show that this larger sample rated as significant nearly all the motivating factors that you had identified from your qualitative study.

Why you might want to do it.

Additional quantitative data that bears out your interpretation of your 'soft' study is very convincing. It is particularly valuable if your clients or examiners are more used to 'hard' research. If you keep the survey format simple and have ready access to a suitable group of respondents, you may be able do this kind of check quickly and cheaply.

It will be much more difficult to use this technique if your findings are sensitive: it could be embarrassing to your informants. It may be technically very difficult or even impossible to get people to confirm a complex story in a simple survey. Think hard before setting up a check that is likely to reject your interpretation.

How to do it.

Firstly, you need to isolate those parts of your interpretation which could be checked in this way. It should be relatively easy to check any lists of apparently significant features, such as problems, tactics or the motivating factors of the example above. Overt behaviours are easier to check than subtle meanings. The more complex, inter-related and subtle the items, the less you can be sure that all your respondents will be interpreting your questions in the same way.

Secondly, you will need to devise a survey. As this is only a check on your main study, you want as simple a format as possible. A single sheet questionnaire, whose results you can tabulate by hand, is probably advisable. You can ask whether or not they recognise each item in their own situation, or they could be asked to rate its importance in their experience 'very important', 'important' or 'not at all important'

Thirdly, you will need a sample of people to fill in your questionnaire. These could be your original informants as described in Item 39: *Checking with informants*. It would be more convincing to go to a larger number of people who are similar to those whom you have studied in depth in your 'soft' study. You might aim at a sample of twenty to thirty respondents. You might take the questionnaire to each one yourself, assure them that they can answer anonymously, and that it will only take them a few minutes to complete. If you have to use the post, there may be long delays and a need for costly reminders. You are bound to get some non-respondents to a postal survey and so you need to take a bigger sample, perhaps forty or fifty, to get a respectable number of replies.

Explain that you are checking out some ideas that you have developed by studying just a few people in depth and that their experience may be different.

43   Showing your credentials

Example.

In the introductory chapter to your report you include a series of sections in which you discuss questions of professional method. These are entitled as follows:

The problem of confidentiality

Measures taken to reduce bias

Measures taken to ensure reliability of categorisation.

Why you might want to do it.

If you can convince your audience that you are a trustworthy researcher, you enable them to pay attention to your findings. You can also avoid unnecessary searches for cosmetic evidence. If you know yourself that you have been appropriately careful and critical throughout your study, you will feel much happier about the whole project.

How to do it.

The key to this approach lies in conveying a self-critical attitude. I see six ways of doing this.

* Show that you have taken problems of confidentiality and your informants' interests seriously.

* Show how you dealt with problems of minimising your influence on the situations you studied.

* Use a sensible selection of techniques to check the evidence and describe this process.

* Discuss alternative interpretations whenever feasible, rather than letting your audience wonder whether you considered them.

* Take a self-critical attitude. I am always suspicious of a perfect or seamless interpretation where all the data clearly support the story and everything that you did turned out for the best.

* If you have done such research before, mention it and consider referring to any efforts that you have made to study soft research methods.

How to present your findings

How to present your findings

What are you trying to do?

You may not need to make a written report of your study at all. It may be enough to become familiar with your data and see what messages it has for your needs. For example, a researcher made a study of mothers' reactions to some Open University materials about childcare. All she wanted to know was whether the mothers liked the materials and whether they used them in any novel ways that had not been anticipated. Her 'report' was an oral assurance to the team who had prepared the materials, saying that all was well and that they should carry on and produce more materials of a similar kind.

However, most of you will have to make a more detailed presentation of your findings than that, whether to colleagues, a client or an examiner, or for your own records.

You will need to show that you have done the work and that your methods were sound. You are trying to give a sense that an appropriate degree of concern for audit informed all that you did. You want to show that your interpretation really does come from your data, rather than out of the air! For some audiences you may also need to justify the qualitative approach and be clear about the generalisability of your findings.

You will almost certainly also need to indicate the context and significance of your findings: how original a contribution do they make to knowledge and what are their implications for your audience?

You have to find a good balance for your report: the appropriate mix of description and interpretation, its implications. You have to solve the problem of what to do about all that data: how to summarise it for the final report.

Whatever the contents of your report, you have to present them in a way that suits your audience. You want to make it easily understood and as useful as possible.

What is this going to be like?

For many people, writing any kind of report, or preparing a talk, is a miserable experience and so they put it off until the deadline is pressing. You may be bursting to talk about your findings, or it may feel like a dreaded ordeal.

When the presentation is made you will almost certainly wish that you had done it differently and will see how your interpretation could have been developed further.

It is also an ending to the project. You will probably feel strong relief at having got there and an urge to congratulate yourself and celebrate. Sometimes I have also felt sad that it is over, having lived with 'my baby' for so long.

So, how can you cope?

The recommended strategy is to **do it as you go along** and build your final presentation from sections drafted during your analysis. In Items 19 to 35, on recognising your own ideas about your data, I suggested a lot of writing and talking to others. If you have done a lot of notes and drafts and explored your ideas in various public forums, you will be in a very strong position for writing a final report. However much drafting you have done, I would urge you to allow more time than you think you need. An unfinished report is rarely acceptable!

Another useful strategy is to **think of your audience**.

* What are their expectations of this presentation?

* What do they know already which you can therefore omit?

* What will their purposes be in paying attention to your presentation?

* What would they really like and what would they hate to find in it?

* What will persuade them to believe you?

* How can you best help them?

Summary

Aims	- Record the work done. - Give a sense of sound methods. - Please your audience.
Feelings	Bursting to tell the world. Jubilation and pride. Facing an ordeal. Relief at finishing. Regrets at what is undone. Sadness at ending.
Strategies	Do it as you go along. Think of your audience.
Techniques	Looking at others' reports. Generalising your findings. Playing critic. Comparisons with quantitative methods. Making a good environment. Preparing in stages. Planning for your audience.

44   Looking at others' reports

Example.

When I was doing my doctoral research, I went to the University of London library to look at successful theses. I asked a librarian for help and she found me several likely looking entries in their index. I studied the thesis titles and sub-titles and asked to see about ten possible theses. Of these about five were sufficiently similar to my kind of work to be worth studying.

Why you might want to do it.

If you cannot immediately see how you wish to present your work, looking at others' reports can save you a lot of time. Even if you do not find a report whose structure you can use unchanged, you should find that this search helps you to see what you do want. It may also remind you of sections that you had forgotten, such as references.

Of course, you cannot always assume that an existing report is a good report but seeing what others get away with can make you feel a lot better!

How to do it.

Look for published and unpublished work in a similar context to your own. Go to a conference to hear soft researchers describing their work. It is more important to see what other researchers have done to satisfy your kind of audience than to find reports on a similar topic. If you are a student nurse presenting a project on nurses as teachers of health education, ask your tutor if you can see other successful project reports, rather than going to a general library looking for research studies on health education.

The kind of questions you want answered might include those that follow.

*   What kind of main sections do they use?

*   Do they include justifications of the methods?

*   How much of the data is included?

*   Is each point made illustrated by data?

* How much checking of the interpretation has been thought necessary?

* How long are they?

* What is in the main body of the presentation and what is in written appendices?

* Do they use diagrams or tables?

* Are they self-critical?

* Do they include ideas which were explored but rejected for the final interpretation?

45   Following the conventions

Example.

A typical qualitative report might include passages such as the following:

'Gender bias appears to affect appointments to senior management positions in a large Health Authority in the South West of England. A 1987 study of practice in Southay Health Authority, Bristol showed that of 23 such appointments, women were successful on only 7 occasions'.

Thus a common pattern in a qualitative report would be:

* Point   ('Gender bias ...etc.')
* Illustrative piece of data ('A 1987 study ..etc.')
* Point
* Illustrative piece of data
* Point
* Illustrative piece of data
* General point (which has no direct data example).

Why you might want to do it.

If you cannot find reports whose structure and conventions are obviously right for your work, then following the above pattern is a pretty safe option.

How to do it.

There are no firm standard conventions, but there are some commonly used structures and ways of dealing with the particular problems of presenting data from soft research.

Start with a section that explains your approach and why you chose it. Item 48: *Comparison with quantitative methods* can be used if you think that that would help. Describe your credentials as an investigator. Explain the precautions you have taken to ensure that your data reflect as normal a situation as possible. Explain your relationship to your informants and whether they knew that you were studying them. Discuss the issue of confidentiality.

It is important to be clear about the four separate kinds of findings:

* Data
* Description
* Interpretation
* Implications.

The simplest thing with the last three of these is to give them separate sections in your report.

With a quantitative study, there tends to be a tradition of placing summary tables of data in an appendix. You can choose to include as an appendix one or two sections of your data, perhaps a whole interview or an account of a meeting in note form. However, one of the most common complaints of examiners about 'soft' research reports is that the interpretation is separate from the data and you cannot see how it was derived from them. You can largely overcome this problem if you intersperse your points of interpretation in the main text with examples from your data. The data acts as a kind of low-level check on the authenticity of your description. You need to avoid long runs of data, which leave all the thinking to the audience, and also long abstract discussions which do not appear to have any basis in experience.

Use some convention to allow your audience to distinguish your words from those of your informants.

Your data is hard to summarise; you must retain the original words of your informants; so you have to select. You will have to decide how much data you want to include. One example for every interpretative category or point that you make is common.

If you plan an oral presentation, remember that a few pages of quotations or written summaries may help your audience.

In selecting from data, you need to look at three criteria:

* The ideal quotation is probably between one line and a third of a page long. Too short and it tells you nothing, too long and it will probably include a lot of distracting material.

* Choose quotations that are typical of the points that you are making. Occasionally you may need to illustrate an important variant, or negative instance but usually you want to avoid examples that are, as it were, 'off-centre', as these will not help the reader to understand your point.

---

* Ideal quotations are well-expressed and striking. Ask yourself whether it will help your audience to feel that they are there in the room, or on the street, with your informants.

Much of the above advice assumes that your data are your informants' words, perhaps transcribed from tape-recordings. However, you may have other kinds of data to include, such as photographs, sketches, diaries, documents, lists or other notes you made while observing, as well as diagrams, and audio or video cassettes.

The key questions to ask yourself about these forms of data are as follows:

* Is it physically feasible to include them in such a way that they will be readily accessible to my audience?

* Will they interest my audience?

* Do they support and illustrate my interpretation?

You may like to include extracts from your diary as described in Item 23: *The researcher's diary* as a final section or appendix.

46   Generalising your findings

Example.

You might have made a study of the loss felt by midwives when mothers die. You might have three instances:
*   The loss of a mother who has become a personal friend.
*   The midwife having lost her fight to save a mother.
*   The midwife's sense of the loss to the family and society.

You might generalise these in less specific categories :
*   Personal friendship loss
*   Work failure
*   Social loss

Why you might want to do it.

You are only likely to want to do this in two situations. The usual reason for generalising is an academic one. If you are a research student, then generalising will be seen as making a greater contribution to the development of academic knowledge. For example, it is not usually any specific occupational group as such that is of interest academically, but rather how consistent they are with theories of behaviour at work. The second reason for generalising is if you have made a study of one situation and want to be asked to go on to study parallel settings. Generalising your findings may help your audience to consider such a possibility.

Generalising will also help you to avoid the criticism that your presentation is too much like journalism. However, generalising without being clear about the limited status of your propositions is dangerous. You must avoid appearing to claim that you have proved anything, or that what you have found definitely applies in other settings.

How to do it.

Look for the terms which are specific to the situations which you have studied and see if you can replace them by more general words. For example, midwives can be relabelled as 'professionals', 'workers' or 'people', and expectant mothers can be called 'patients' or 'people'. Obviously, you need to consider the sensibilities of your audience, which may include some of your informants. Midwives would not be happy to have their experience generalised as 'nursing' and there is heated debate about calling patients 'clients'. You must also avoid silly jargon. For example, do not call the postman's sorting of letters 'a guided option management strategy'!

Another approach is to ask yourself whether similar situations exist in other settings. If you can think of a few parallel situations, see how you could redraft your interpretation so that it could be read as applying to all those situations. Until you actually try is easy to imagine you cannot do this. In considering the 'midwives loss' example quoted above, you might gain insights beneficial for your research by comparison with other situations: a gardener losing a valued plant, a lawyer losing a court case and a businessman losing an important contract. Of course you must remain aware of the different orders of experience involved.

When you present your interpretation, you may like to treat it on two levels:

*   Your interpretation of the the story behind your description of your data.

*   The more generalised version of the story.

and tell your audience when you are going to do this.

In presenting a further level of generalisation, you must limit your claims. YOUR INTERPRETATION IS PERSONAL TO YOU AND APPLIES ONLY TO THE SETTING IN WHICH YOU MADE YOUR STUDY. The generalised interpretation is put forward as a hypothesis, to indicate how your study might fit into work in other contexts and to suggest ideas that could be explored in other contexts.

47   Playing critic

Example.

When I was a student doing my first piece of 'soft' research I went to several tutors who had experience with these kind of projects. I asked them what were the common failings of qualitative reports. I also read some more critical studies of similar research.

Why you might want to do it.

If you know how your audience is likely to criticise your work, you can prepare to meet their comments positively and creatively. The behaviour of being your own critic also shows your audience a flavour of audit in your presentation consistent with Item 43: *Showing your credentials.*

How to do it.

Here is a list of common criticisms made by clients and supervisors of soft research, with some suggestions of how to defend yourself against them. You need to think which of these criticisms might be made by your audience. Then consider whether your study can be criticised on those grounds. Consider whether presenting your work differently could help. With any remaining criticisms that you feel are valid, consider whether it is worth doing more work to defuse them. If there is no way of remedying the situation, then raise the criticism yourself in your report.

* 'There is no 'real' data in the report, only the researcher's summaries or descriptions of 'typical' people.'
  Suggestions on how to include your data can be found in item 45, *Follow the conventions.*

* 'There is too much 'raw' data, with not enough analysis.'
  It would be rare for a report in which more than half the pages were reproducing the data to be appreciated.

* 'The interpretation is separate from the data and does not appear to arise from it.'
  Even if you have developed the interpretation from the data, it may not show that you have, if you fail to illustrate your points. It may be worth considering item 39 *Checking with your informants* , if you are unable to find convincing data.

* 'There is inappropriate quantification.'
  Some critics want to know that you have counted instances and negative instances of every point that you make but more will probably find this kind of presentation inappropriate for qualitative research on a small sample. Look at other ways of providing evidence in items 36 to 43.

* 'The interpretation contains nothing new.'
  Academic critics especially may complain about this if your report is for a higher degree. They are particularly likely to get irritated if you give new names to old ideas without acknowledging the existing literature. Check why you felt that your study was worth undertaking. Try item 27 *Seminars,* to see if other people can see anything new in your findings.

* 'The relevant literature is summarised but then the rest of the report fails to make any reference or links to that set of existing ideas, even in the concluding section.'
  The missing link can often be provided by identifying a series of predictions that the authors of the relevant literature would make to your area of study.

* 'The interpretation is too simple.' (or too complex).
  Unless it is a very brief exploratory project, categories at a single level are probably inadequate. For example, finding six types of student behaviour. Similarly, two main categories each with two sub-divisions, seems a bit thin. On the other hand enormously elaborated interpretations, with many levels and lots of different kinds of concepts, can all get too confusing, especially if there is no overview or model of their inter-relationships.

* 'The categories are not defined, even if they are illustrated.'
  Work out how you would describe each to a second categoriser as in Item 37 or try out definitions on friends.

* 'The researchers make too sweeping claims for their findings, forgetting that their interpretation can only be a personal one and limited to the situation they studied.'
  Use Item 46: *Generalising your categories.*

* 'The researcher is insufficiently objective, showing her dislike of what she found.'
  Consider cutting any evaluative statements. However, if the work is aimed at a practical outcome, it may be appropriate to identify what you see as problems and to suggest ameliorative action. Avoid direct criticism of your audience in all cases.

48   Comparison with quantitative methods

Example.

In a study of occupational therapists for clients who were used to quantitative studies of manpower, you might have to justify your approach by emphasising the need for new insights. You would point out how a quantitative approach would make this aim difficult to achieve. You might also argue that quantitative studies were unlikely to be viewed with enthusiasm at a time when, as the profession was struggling with many other demands for hard data on their work and viewed quantitative manpower studies with suspicion.

Why you might want to do it.

You may have done 'soft' research for all sorts of reasons, such as a dislike of quantitative methods or a desire to focus on a single case study to avoid travelling. Unless you were **asked** to use qualitative methods, you will probably need to justify and explain this decision. This will be particularly necessary if the readers of your report are going to be surprised by this approach and potentially critical of it. If they tend to value 'hard, scientific' research and talk of reliability a lot, then you will need to explain your approach very carefully.

It can be very powerful if you feel able to be critical of your choice of approach to the research. It defuses criticism and shows confidence. You may also be able to impress by your grasp of the complex arguments involved.

How to do it.

There are two useful ideas to make the centre of your points. The first is that 'soft' research is good for validity and the second is that it is good for exploring the unknown. Your arguments can focus on both the failings of quantitative methods and the advantages of the qualitative approach.

On validity, the argument is essentially that by studying a few informants in depth in as near as possible to their normal settings, you have a good chance of producing ideas that are close to reality. Quantitative methods are closer to experiments, and tend by their nature to isolate parts of behaviour and ask people about their perceptions of events at times when they are not involved in those events. In that kind of research one is studying only surrogates: simple models of situations and not the situations themselves.

Quantitative methods rely on having ideas to test and consequently on the quality of those initial ideas. That is a reasonable approach for a situation that is well understood; it is unreasonable for topics which have been little studied.

Try to be self-critical: do not list only the arguments that favour your choice of methods, but explore its weaknesses too. Most should be outweighed by the strengths of the method.

49   Making a good environment

Example.

One author that I know often begins any serious piece of writing by inscribing a favourite poem in beautiful thick black ink on a clean white sheet of paper. Once the poem is completed and on top of his pile of paper, he feels more able to take up a biro and start drafting his technical report. Later he removes the sheet with the poem from the front of his work.

Why you might want to do it.

Many people dislike writing or suffer from 'writer's block'. Attention to your writing environment can help you to overcome the emotional barriers and enjoy it more. The tricks on starting seem to help the many people who have trouble with that initial hurdle.

How to do it.

First of all find a good place to write. For most people this means somewhere private and quiet, preferably where they can leave their work untouched for several days if necessary. I often write in a double bed, with all my notes spread out around me. It seems to prevent me from getting up and wandering off!

You may like to invest in good quality paper and coloured pens, black ink or whatever seems luxurious and attractive to you. I like to work on a word processor, but only if I can print a paper copy frequently and conveniently.

Try the trick of writing something irrelevant but satisfying on the top sheet, like the poem in the example above, if you are reluctant to begin.

Having a pile of clean 3" by 4" cards can enable you to begin work without really feeling that you are 'writing'. Similarly, you don't have to draft a report in writing at all. You may prefer to draft onto audio-cassettes, or go for a walk and declaim sentences into the air.

If you have access to a word processor, remember that you can make it check your spelling, move paragraphs around and delete sections at will. You do not have to wait until you have finished to print out a paper copy of what you have done. Take copies every time you add or alter more than a couple of pages, so that you can look at it as a whole and gain a sense of progress. You may have a desk-top publishing package or be able to get some advice on how to print a copy that looks good, with printed graphics, a smart title page and coloured cover. You can also save alternative versions of your text and only decide which one you prefer later: you don't have to 'delete' until you are ready.

I found that many of the academics that I studied rewarded themselves for writing on a piecework basis. They would promise themselves a walk or a cup of coffee after every few pages were completed.

50 Preparing in stages

Example.

When I was preparing an article about my doctoral research, I divided the work as follows.

* I made some notes and talked these over out loud to myself, trying to discover the most important things that I wanted to say.

* I drafted the article, trying only to get the main points down in a sensible order and in words that made sense to me. I kept changing the 'contents' list' as I did this.

* Then I considered my readers and redrafted the article to be clearer and more useful.

* Finally, I crawled through it, copy-editing to improve the grammar, spelling and punctuation. I thought about layout, the spacing of headings and the design of the tables.

Why you might want to do it.

If you focus on the whole product all the time you will probably find its preparation hard. The task is too complex: you are trying to reconcile often conflicting demands from your material, your own wishes, your views of your audience and conventions on presentation, down to the level of how long should a paragraph be, or when to show the slides in a lecture. There are just too many criteria to hold in your head at once.

How to do it.

You may have been taught a system at school of planning by making a set of notes and then writing each section in turn, starting with the introduction. However, it is now known that not everyone is best suited to that process and it seems helpful to LET YOURSELF EXPERIMENT AND FIND A PROCESS THAT SUITS YOU. A neat plan, followed by sequential drafting, is very unusual behaviour among experienced writers or speakers.

Remember that you do not have to begin at the beginning. Many researchers find it easier to draft some sections of their report than others, so start there and fill in the rest later. Others find that they need to externalise the whole thing before they can plan a sensible order for its presentation to an audience. It is only in writing or talking about their findings, in detail, that they discover what they want to present.

When you feel that you are ready to work on your presentation I suggest that you list all the jobs that have to be done. Then group them, so that you can tackle them a few at a time. Here is a possible list for a lengthy written report.

*   Brainstorm: jot down all the points you want to make, in any order.

*   Sort out the main messages that you want to put over.

*   Create a good environment for the writing.

*   Sequence your planned content and group your ideas under headings.

*   Express the ideas in words that make sense to you.

*   Check that draft against your expectations of your readers.

*   Edit your words so that they flow better.

*   Add illustrations: data and diagrams.

*   Consider layout and add sub-headings for greater clarity and accessibility.

*   Check your grammar, spelling and punctuation.

*   Decide on type faces.

*   Make a plan for the distribution of your report and draft any covering letters.

Another way of dividing up the process is to see it as three stages, each with a focus on a different group of people.

Stage 1   Preparing a presentation for yourself. Sorting out your ideas and getting out the points that you feel are important, in words that make sense to you.

Stage 2   Redrafting to suit your colleagues. Defining your terms and adding sections to explain things that you take for granted. Subtracting sections that you now see are only personal interests of yours.

Stage 3   Redrafting for a wider audience. This may involve some more work on clarity and also focussing on their expectations about written or spoken presentations. Problems may also arise from having to reduce or expand the length of the piece, short or uncertain deadlines, quirks of publishers, and the uncertainty of facilities in lecture rooms.

Another way of dividing up the process is to see it as going through different media stages.

* You begin by making notes.

* You discuss these notes with your boss.

* You draft a contents list in a sequence, i.e. a paper plan.

* You prepare notes on index cards for each of the sections of your plan.

* You dictate a version for your secretary to type onto a micro-computer.

* You print a copy and edit on that paper copy.

* Your secretary turns that into a polished report using a desk-top publishing package on her micro-computer.

However you decide to tackle the work, by dividing it up or by progressive refocussing, I suggest that there are two essential steps.

* Check your draft with someone else. Get comments on it.

* Distance yourself at least once during the preparation, by taking several days away from it. You need to see the whole with fresh eyes.

`1   Planning for your audience

Example.

In this book I have tried to anticipate your needs and to address the questions that are most likely to concern you. I have used direct questions as headings in my descriptions. I have used a standard layout for each technique to help you to find your way about. I have treated each technique separately and provided a contents list to help you to dip into those parts you want without having to read through the whole book.

Why you might want to do it.

It is easy to lose sight of this while doing the research, but presumably your main reason for all this work is to have some effect on a wider audience than yourself. I want my work to be readily understood and I want my audience to react in the way I want. Personally I also want feedback from an audience and I want that feedback to be as complimentary as possible.

How to do it.

You need to work out what your readers really want to know and how best to put it to them. Try to answer the questions in Item 28: *Visualising your audience.* Even if you think you know the answers it is probably worth checking them with one or two members of your audience. Ask yourself the following questions.

*   Will they understand that?

*   Do they really need me to tell them that?

*   What will persuade them to my views of this?

When you come to consider sequencing and layout of a written report, try to make life as easy as possible for your readers. Use the suggestions in Item 27: *Seminars to improve an oral presentation.*

For a written report try the following.

*   Use an open layout, grouping related paragraphs closer together and leaving a wide space before a new section.

---

*   Think of a sentence as a single idea and a paragraph as a small group of closely related points.

*   If you are unsure how to punctuate your work, you might be helped by reading what you have written aloud, as if to a large audience. Where you take a breath, you need to insert some punctuation!

*   Unless your audience insists on a formal style, a simple direct style is better. Write ' did...' not 'The researcher did...'

*   Avoid jargon, unnecessarily abstract terms and long words which have simpler shorter versions.

*   Try to make the verbs active and avoid the passive tense. Write 'The student thumped the table...' rather than 'The table was thumped by the student...'

*   Short sentences and short commonly used words are easier to read. You might like to check the 'readability' of your normal style of writing using the process described below. It is a rough measure, but if you score over 35 using this method it would be worth trying to simplify your style even for a professional audience. Lay readers are better served by a score under 25, and can get help with achieving this by reference to G. R Wainwright's *People and Communication*.

These are the stages of the 'readability' check:

1   Mark off a 100 word typical sample of your writing. N.B. Numbers and symbols are counted as short words, hyphenated words are counted as two words.

2   Count the number of complete sentences in the sample.

3   Count the number of words in the complete sentences (I usually do it by subtracting the words left over from 100).

4   Work out the average sentence length by dividing the answer for step 3 by the answer for step 2.

5   Count the number of words of more than two syllables in the full 100 word sample. Do not count names which start with a capital letter. (A syllable is a vowel sound, so

'advised' has 2 syllables, 'advisable' has 3.)

6   Add the answers for steps 4 and 5. This is your test score. If it is too high for your
     audience, start by dividing each sentence into two and see if you can replace any of
     your long words with shorter ones.

Reference

Gordon R Wainwright   *People and Communication*
                             Macdonald & Evans 1979

Selecting techniques

52   The need to select techniques

On any single study you would be unlikely to use more than ten of the fifty-odd techniques described in this book. For example, in my study of Health Authority members I had interview data recorded in hand-written notes. I used only a single **organisational technique**.

*   Item 10: *Adding your own comments*
     I added my thoughts in brackets as I scribbled my notes.

In order to **hear what my data had to say**, I chose to use three techniques.

*   Item 11: *Go back and get more data* where I found gaps in the biographical material that I needed.

*   Item 12: *Written summaries*. I transferred the points from each interview onto topic cards as cryptic notes in tiny writing.

*   Item 13: *Looking for common points*. I read through each card in turn, looking for points which had support from several members.

I found my own **ideas about what my data had to say** by using two techniques.

*   Item 20: *Self-interrogation*. I asked myself *What is really important in all this?* and *What do I really want to say to them?*

*   Item 28: *Visualising your audience*. I asked myself *What are they expecting me to say and do?* and later *If I say these are my findings, how will they react?*

I did not use any particular techniques to **organise the evidence for this interpretation** or to present my findings. When I described my conclusions to my informants, who were the clients for this piece of work, I asked them to take my word that I was reporting back my perception of their views. I asked them to look around the group, for I was relying on the expressions on their faces to provide the evidence for my interpretations.

On the much larger study for my doctoral research I used more of the 'playing' techniques, but I was selective about the 'housekeeping'. I used about half the data organising techniques and half the ways of organising evidence for my interpretation. Since original ideas were a key criterion for judging such research, I tried every single one of the techniques in the sections **How to hear what your data has to say** and **How to recognise and pattern your own ideas about our data** for exploring the data and its meaning.

Some of them, of course, proved much more useful than others.

53   How to select techniques

I have four criteria for the selection of techniques.

*   What do the data suggest?

*   What is feasible?

*   How good has it got to be?

*   What do you like doing?

What do the data suggest?
The first criterion comes from the form and amount of your data. Most techniques can only be done on written data and many are not needed for small amounts of data. There seems little point in choosing over-elaborate techniques for your study. For example, I could have taped and transcribed my interviews with health authority members, asked my secretary to put them on the computer and used a word search programme for my initial analysis. I believe that the simpler techniques that I chose saved a lot of time with little loss of information. However, a few pages of data can be a gold-mine if you want to focus on it. I shall never forget giving out copies of two pages of a transcript of a meeting to a group of ten social scientists. It held so many different concepts and interpretations for them that they were ale to discuss the data for two hours.

What is feasible?
The second criterion is about resources: time, money and facilities. Have you got good access to a micro-computer? Can you get someone to make typed transcripts of audio-cassettes? Can you afford an assistant's time to act as second categoriser? Have you the money for a quantitative survey to check your results? Do you work in a team that can bounce ideas off each other?

How good has it got to be?
The third criterion is about your aims. Textbooks tend to suggest that there is only one standard of professional work. I disagree. I have found that some studies are best left at the descriptive surface stage while others require deep thought and a creative approach to the search for the underlying meanings. Ask yourself about your role as the researcher an about the audience's expectations. Are you researching to check or illustrate ideas, to sensitise an audience to your informants' situation, to develop categories for a subsequent quantitative survey or to find new

hypotheses? Are you independent of your audience or employed by your client to help them achieve their ends, regardless of your own views? Are you out to understand or to change things? Does your audience need a strong sense of attention to evidence and audit? Does it demand a good story?

What do you like doing?

The final criterion pays attention to your own preferences. I have found that I can trust my instincts to tell me when I am spending an inappropriate amount of energy on an unhelpful technique. If I feel irritated then I need to question what I am doing. Of course, sometimes I feel the work is boring but that I am making progress and then I know that it is worth persevering a while longer.

I also have a strong preference for drawing diagrams and talking ideas out loud, with or without an audience! You may know that you prefer working in teams, or on a word processor, or that you enjoy writing. Choose techniques that allow for your strengths and you will produce better work, faster and with more satisfaction.

My good wishes go with you!

ORDER FORM

Please supply: Quantity   Price   Total

	Quantity	Price	Total
Preparing To Teach	.....	£7.95	....
53 Interesting Things To Do In Your Lectures	.....	£6.95	....
53 Interesting Things To Do In Your Seminars And Tutorials	.....	£6.95	....
53 Interesting Ways To Assess Your Students	.....	£6.95	....
53 Interesting Ways Of Helping Your Students To Study	.....	£7.95	....
53 Interesting Communication Exercises For Science Students	.....	£7.95	....
53 Interesting Ways To Appraise Your Teaching	.....	£7.95	....
53 Interesting Ways To Promote Equal Opportunities in Education	.....	£7.95	....
253 Ideas For Your Teaching	.....	£6.95	....
7 Do-it-yourself Training Exercises	.....	£6.95	....
Creating A Teaching Profile	.....	£5.95	....
Getting the most from your data. *Practical ideas on how to analyse qualitative data*	.....	£8.95	....

Total cost of books ordered   £   :

Plus postage and packing (add 10%)   £   :

Total   £   :

(Please tick relevant box)

☐ I enclose a cheque for £   :   payable to Plymbridge Dist. Ltd.
☐ I have paid via National Giro to Plymbridge acc. no. 221 2951

☐ Please charge credit card:

Access ☐	Barclaycard ☐	Diners Club ☐
Visa ☐	Mastercard ☐	American Express ☐

Expiry date ....

Card Number ☐☐☐☐   ☐☐☐☐   ☐☐☐☐   ☐☐☐☐

Name ....

Address ....

....

.... Postcode ....

Signature ....

Send your order form to: Plymbridge Distributors Ltd.
                             Estover Road,   Plymouth,   PL6 7PZ
                             ☎ 0752 705251   Fax 0752 777 603

90/4